J. Perkins Tracy

The Tourists Companion and Guide to Coney Island, Fort Hamilton, Bath Beach, Sheepshead Bay, Rockaway Beach and Far Rockaway

J. Perkins Tracy

The Tourists Companion and Guide to Coney Island, Fort Hamilton, Bath Beach, Sheepshead Bay, Rockaway Beach and Far Rockaway

ISBN/EAN: 9783337478285

Printed in Europe, USA, Canada, Australia, Japan

Cover: Foto ©Andreas Hilbeck / pixelio.de

More available books at **www.hansebooks.com**

THE

TOURISTS COMPANION

AND

GUIDE

TO

Coney Island, Fort Hamilton, Bath Beach,

SHEEPSHEAD BAY,

ROCKAWAY BEACH AND FAR ROCKAWAY,

TO WHICH IS ADDED

A Description of Public Buildings, Famous Landmarks, Parks, Churches, Theatres,
Libraries, Art Galleries and other matters of interest to Strangers,
in the City New York and vicinity,

EDITED BY

J. PERKINS TRACY.

—— • ❖ • ——

A SELECT BUSINESS DIRECTORY

of each place noticed in the pages of this Guide.

NEW YORK:

AUSTIN PUBLISHING CO., PUBLISHERS,

7 MURRAY STREET.

ONG ISLAND, whose "sea-girt shore" stretches for one hundred and twenty-five miles along the Atlantic coast, has, within the last fifteen years, come rapidly into prominence as the great watering district of the American continent ; and probably no territory, from Baffin Bay to Terra del Fuego, presents attributes for the establishment of summer resorts to so great a degree as this Island whereof we speak.   From the village of Bath to Montauk Point, the southern shore is almost one unbroken sandy beach, where the bather can plunge in the surf and frolic among the breakers to his heart's content ; whilein the many beautiful inlets and bays on the northern side the more timid can lave in placid waters, and dip in the salt sea without the many misgivings awakened by the roar and foam of the billowy Atlantic.

To wade upon the silvery sands at Orient, to stroll along the pebbly strands of Peconic Bay, or saunter amid the boulders and cliffs of Montauk, and listen to the wild sea waves, is delightful beyond measure.   To ramble throughout the diversified landscapes and picturesque scenery of the interior ; its pastoral fields ; its beautiful villas ; its hills and dales ; its dells and dingles ; its rills and rivulets ; to loiter by its babbling brooks, and hearken to the murmurings of their rippling waters, to cull the flowers that blossom on their borders, to angle on their shingly bottoms, while the melodies of woodland song-birds are warbled in your ear, is enchantment to even the most prosaic mind. Relaxation from the cares, toil, struggles and turmoil of the city life can nowhere be more keenly enjoyed than on this arcadia by the sea.

When the days grow hotter inland; when the dust of July begins to settle in the streets of the great city, and the nights become more and more insufferable, here along the coast the even-tempered breezes charm away the heat. The pure salt breath of the ocean as it greets you is a tonic invitation to resist depression and decay. The resistless, eternal splash of the waves—the deep blue waves—suggest power with ease and beauty, as each scattered drop is gathered and dashed again and again at your feet. Your prompted energies quicken and revive; you realize to the full, intensities of expression. You are delighted with the briskness of life; the exhilarating air; the marked sense of health; the gay colors which are so agreeable in the cool shadows of the afternoon; the faint sound of music and the sea; the laughter of children —all this, and more, come to you with the freshness of a new world. For this you have forsaken a sunburnt city; baked and dusty sidewalks; languid streets; a marked sense of physical depression; people with fever in their faces and dejection in their walk; where there is no sound of music, except it be the monotonous strains of a German band before a beer saloon. Who would not exchange such a metropolis for the sea?

Thus, gentle reader, are you invited to partake of the advantages lying at your very door. Thus we tempt you to the gaiety of Coney Island and Rockaway Beach, and to the solid comforts and pleasures of the many other summer watering places along the southern shore of Long Island, a description of, and a truthful guide to which, it is the purpose of this little work to furnish.

CONEY ISLAND.

ON the south-western extremity of Long Island, where the waters of the noble Hudson flow through the lower New York Bay to join the ocean, is situated this now celebrated summer resort. Beginning at Gravesend Bay it presents, for five miles in an easterly direction, a gradual sloping beach, where thousands of New Yorkers, as well as visitors from other places in the vicinity, enjoy the caresses of the old Atlantic. From the eastern end of the island—what was once known as Pelican Beach, now Manhattan Beach, and where snipe, plover and other game were then plentiful—projects a narrow point of sand, forming a bay famous as a fishing place, called Sheepshead Bay, after the delicious fish of that name which in remote ages was supposed to have harbored within its borders. From Sheepshead Bay in a westerly direction runs Coney Island Creek to Gravesend Bay, thus making the circuit of the island—a barren, sandy waste metamorphosed by capital and enterprise into an island of enchantment, so far as enchantment is compatable with business principles.

In former years the attractions that lured visitors to Coney Island were tame when compared with those set forth in such tempting array to-day. Let it not be supposed that the only happiness at the sea-side centres on hotel porches and in cottage parlors; that the human life when upon the piers and beaches furnishes all there is of interest. The flat, sandy shore is itself a world of wonders, and has a life of its own. Prof. Joseph Leidy, who is so well known for his accuracy of research, found in an ounce of sand collected between high and low tide more than 28,000 minute shells. Does not this open the gate to hours of delightful interest? For shells have long excited attention. A shell hunt along the wild and sandy shore of the Island was one of the exhilarating pastimes of "ye olden time."

In those days the beach was reached in a dilapidated steamer, and the crowd on board was never so large but that one had plenty of elbow room. Arrived on the Island the attractions offered were a dash in the surf, a promenade on the shore, a carousal, the bracing sea breeze, and a good fish or clam dinner at the hostelries, if the unpretending sheds, where good fish and bad whisky were dispensed, could be dignified by such a title. These places were few in number and situated toward the west end. The entertainment they offered was not calculated to please the fastidious taste ; the dainty found no morsel to their liking, and the elite, when they sought the pleasures of the Island, enjoyed them *sub rosa*. Wyckoff, Van Sicklen, Felter and Rodger were the famous publicans of the time. Wyckoff was admitted to be pioneer ; but it was a matter of contention which was " King of Coney Island." They all reigned by turns, 'tis believed, although History has neglected to chronicle the realm in this regard.

During midsummer, when old Sol tormented the busy denizens of the metropolis with his unremitting rays, as many as a thousand persons have at one time sought the cool comfort of the seaside ; but generally the excursionists numbered much less. During these summer afternoons life and merriment prevailed. An impromptu dance at the hotels to the music of a fiddle was the Terpsichorean feature ; and a stray trio of Ethiopian minstrels, with banjo, bones and tambourine, or an itinerant piper, harpest or violinist furnished the orchestral display.

Adjacent to the hotels were rows of bathing-houses, looking like rickety sentry boxes, for the accommodation of bathers, to be hired, including towel and bathing clothes, for twenty-five cents for each person.

After all the wide, deep blue expanse of sea was the chief attraction ; and in what element is there more romance, for in its depths rest the wrecks of "ten thousand royal argosies." Homer often speaks of "the wine-faced deep :" and a modern English poet tells of "Summer isles of Eden lying in the dark purple spheres of sea." In truth, a purplish or wine-like flush may at times be noticed on the ocean under peculiar atmospheric conditions. More often it is sea-green when the winds are fresh and the skies are overcast. A dark-gray prevails when a storm is at hand. Near California there is a "Vermilion" sea, which at times presents a very reddish tint. The ocean near Key West is of a milky hue, owing to the great banks of white coral at the sea-bottom. Yet none of these colors equal the blue of the sea at Coney Island on a rare day in June. Toward nights its tints grow darker and more blue, and the horizon in the light of the setting sun seems just a line of black, beaded with burning gold. That fades at last, and a loiterer can but listen and—

> " Here the grating roar
> Of pebbles which the waves strike back, and fling
> At their return up the high strand,
> Begin and cease ; and then again begin,
> With tremulous cadence slow, and bring
> The eternal note of sadness in. "

The waves upon the Coney Island beach have embraced thousands of people since those early days when the sands were innocent of the gaudy catch-pennys that now flaunt their alluring attractions before the public eye ; and to-day these self-same waves beat as musically and as endlessly, and break into as many lines of foam, as they did before the Island became a prey to the mammon-loving invader. Indeed, in spite of the allurements of this Vanity Fair by the sea, the waves are still one of the standard attractions of Coney Island. Watching, you are tempted to speculate concerning them. They are very beautiful. As they rise in gallant shape far out, topped by crests of white, they seem to be race-horses with wild and flowing manes. Then they break, and with a roar of exultation toss themselves upon the floor of whitened sand.

But to continue our retrospect. From a point in the town of Gravesend, adjacent to where is now located the Prospect Park Fair Grounds, ran the Shell road, the popular drive to Coney Island, and for years the only approach to the frequented portion of the beach available for vehicles. This road was from the city by two avenues, namely : the Fort Hamilton Road and the Flatbush Turnpike, equally pleasant routes. The former presented a full view of New

York Bay, and the latter passed through a fertile district abounding in quaint old homesteads, neat cottages and well planted gardens. By the way of Fort Hamilton, we went through State Lane—in the town of New Utrecht—by the old stone church (still standing), at the junction of the Bath and New Utrecht roads, to the King's Highway, thence to the "Old Shell Road." By the Turnpike, we passed over Prospect Hill, paid toll at Valley Grove, rode through the villages of Flatbush and Flatlands, through the town of Gravesend to Shell Road, over the bridge at Coney Island Creek, to the beach.

The Fort Hamilton Road was the choice of New Yorkers, the Turnpike of Brooklynites, though the faces of many old-time sports from both cities, since gone "over to the majority," were familiar on both roads; so, too, like the many kindly spirits that were wont to enliven the scenes with their jolly presence, has the glory of the old roads departed, and where once the fleet trotter coursed over graveled roadbeds, the rumble of the dray, and the thud of the truck, is heard on heavy pavements; and even the "Old Shell Road" echoes the snort of the "Iron Horse."

In more recent years Coney Island Road was opened, and travel to the beach deserted the old for the new road, which became the popular drive to the shore, and so remained until about the year 1858, when it was given over to the horse railroad. On the completion of the boulevard known as the Ocean Park Way, Coney Island Road passed from existence as a drive.

For several years prior to 1874 the Island was but little patronized by the better classes, owing to the difficulty of reaching it, and the reputation for disorder which it obtained through various causes. In 1874 a steam road from 20th Street, Brooklyn, was built by an enterprising capitalist to what is now known as West Brighton Beach, and a large pavilion and restaurant were erected at its terminus. The result proved that the enterprise necessary to afford a convenient means of reaching the Island was all that was necessary to secure for the place the position to which its location and natural advantages entitled it, as the most popular watering place in this country. In 1875 a syndicate secured control of the eastern end, or Manhattan Beach, and erected thereon the mammoth hotel that was opened in 1877.

Manhattan Hotel.

The plan for the development of Manhattan Beach embraced the building of a railroad connecting New York city
with that place; and so quietly and unostentatiously were
these plans matured, that the hotel and the railway with their
appurtenances were completed before the general public was
aware that even the construction of so important an undertaking was contemplated. Minerva-like it came into existence
"all armed and ready for the fray," if we may be permitted
to use that phrase to express the friendly contact that took
place during the opening season between the thousands of
visitors, and the projectors of the enterprise.

The successes at Manhattan Beach gave an impetus to
other sections of the island; other railroad facilities were constructed; spacious hotels and minor places of amusement
sprung up in all directions; excellent police protection was
inaugurated; the rowdy element was forced to succumb to law
and order; and that prosperity, unexampled in the history of
watering-places, was begun that has made "Coney Island" as
familiar as a household word in every portion of the land.

It is estimated that at least 40,000 persons visit the Island
daily, from the opening of the season on June 1st, to the
close thereof in October; and that on holidays, special oc-
casions and Sundays, the number often exceeds 100,000.
It is an interesting diversion to watch the incongruous multitude of pleasure-seekers abroad in every direction upon the
sands. The phlegmatic Teuton with his family well provided with lunch baskets; the genial Hibernian with *his*
family bent upon a good time; the complaisant French-
man, strolling pleasantly along , the dudish cockney, with his
abreviated coat-tails, la-da-da cane and insipient moustache;
the lank, calculating Yankee, with an eye to future spoils;
the sandy Scotchman, the dark-skinned Italian gentleman of
means; the well-dressed negro, bent upon a lark and bound
to have it; the banker, the governor, the "well-heeled" al-
derman; the simpering maid and stately matron; the happy
benedict and the crabbed bachelor; the lovers, seeing romance in the sea and poetry in life; the prattling, romping
merry groups of children. Here the elements of human nature do most beautifully compound. The young, the old,
the fat, the lean, the short, the tall, the dull, the gay, resort
to relieve the tedium of city life—to woo the balmy breezes
and frolic in the surf.

No little inducement at the Island is the magnitude and variety of the cuisine—anything in the edible line, from the sandwich to a banquet, can be had at reasonable prices. The daintiest tidbits for those of delicate taste, and the most substantial solids for voracious appetites, (for the sea air is no common appetizer) are always ready, and in constant demand. Hence, a visit to the Island and a feast, be it but a clam chowder, is one and inseperable. As a dry meal is but an aggravation, the thoughtful caterers provide lists of liquid essentials, ranging from "extra dry" Heidsick to the discreet soda water; but the "King pin" of all in point of ready sale is that most democratic of all drinks, the "foaming glass of beer," and therefore no one need go dry while he has five cents in his pocket.

Though the prices for refreshments are not excessive (indeed, one may procure an excellent table d'hote for a dollar), yet there are many who patronize the Island whose purse will not keep pace with their wants in this direction. This generally applies to the humble paterfamilias, with a large and growing family, who is forever at his wit's end to eke out a respectable living with the fruits of a slender salary. Therefore, in the cause of economy, he must needs prepare a hamper at home, that the family be sufficiently provided with lunch at the seashore. Then, too, there are others who prefer this method from choice. For these classes there are ample a commodations in every locality of the Island ; places where tables and seats are set aside for this very purpose, known as "basket" places, and where milk, hot tea and coffee, and other drinkables can be obtained. Indeed, 'tis often a pleasant sight to watch the family group taking their frugal repast, and observe the gusto with which the little ones enjoy the good things "mama" has provided.

The conveyances for the transit of passengers between the different parts of the Island are numerous, and being constantly in motion, add to the continuous bustle, so noticeable and attractive to the stranger. You have your choice of stage, carryall or barouche, not to speak of the Marine Railway. The fare is moderate, and you have no excuse at all for leg weariness. They that prefer the promenade can enjoy it without discomfort, for a broad plankway skirts Surf Avenue, within a stone's throw of the water, and one need not make a toil of pleasure by trudging through the sand.

Nowhere else in the world are the facilities for bathing equal to those of the Island. Large commodious structures, complete in every accommodation, and conducted in the most proper manner, with all the auxiliaries for sea bathing, are at the public's service, at moderate rates. Around the bathing places are constantly gathered crowds of people, enjoying the antics of the bathers ; and truly these spots afford a great deal of fun for both on-lookers as well as those in the water. Here you can see the timid maiden shivering at the water's edge, ere she can be persuaded to wade forward to meet the on-coming wave from which she presently flies with a little shriek of fancied terror. Yonder a stout lady is seen waddling down to the sea in happy consciousness that no wave can upset her equilibrium ; and striking terror to the souls of the lean young men and women about whose padless limbs their tights hang in dejected folds. Then there is the facetious individual who talks at the spectators ; and the athletic young man who poses with apparent unconsciousness that many pairs of eyes are " taking in " the striking symmetry of his well-rounded figure ; and the gay and festive bald-headed merchant who feels as gleeful as a schoolboy out on a lark, as he approaches the surf ; and the dashing, coquettish beauty, in her dainty costume, abreviated as much as custom permits, who flashes past like a brilliant butterfly, and is presently frolicking amid the waves. What playful shrieks and rippling laughter float upon the air ; what a splashing and ducking ; what a scampering along the wet shore ; what an air of intense enjoyment is here to be observed ! And this is an every day sight during the warm summer months. At night, under the rays of the electric light, the scene is even more picturesque ! The looker-on can form illusions of dolphins and mermaids, nymphs and perii, and fancy himself in the realms of the Naiads.

The lovers of music (is there a soul so cheerless that hath no ear for melody ?) will find delight in the afternoon and evening concerts given at the grand music stands of the principal hotels. The performers are selected with the greatest care, and the rivalry to secure the best musical talent results (much to the public's benefit) in the organization of orchestras of great merit, and led as they are by virtuosos of celebrity, present a repertory of original and selected compositions that never fail to gain the plaudits and appreciation of the multitude; indeed, the most critical philharmonist seldom finds occasion to speak other than praise of these concerts by the sea.

Truly there is no lack of music on the Island, but we will not say that you will find harmony everywhere. Nearly every shanty that caters to the public taste, is provided with some kind of musical adjunct to beguile the pleasure seeker. It may be in the shape of an imitation negro in a "loud" suit and a gigantic collar, who twangs the banjo; or a hollow-eyed young man who seems engaged at a game of fisty cuffs with a consumptive piano; or a trio of pasty-faced Germans, who are extracting noise from an asthmatic cornet, cracked-toned flageolet, and a very much abused trombone; or a couple of seedy Italians wrestling with a harp and violin, with perhaps the addition of a little girl or boy, with a triangle; or again it may be a very primitive orchestra of five or six performers (Heaven save the mark!) Then if you dote on vocal music, why drop in at one of the beer caravansaries, and behold, you will have anything from the soul-stirring strain of "Nancy Lee" to the latest of Harrigan's eccentricities, but not one after the fashion of Mr. Harrigan himself—no, these performers have a style peculiar to themselves, which they are proud to think superior even to the original. Indeed, their grotesque humor is of the most spontaneous description, so that it is not to be wondered at if many simple folk fondly believe that they (the performers) are really funny.

All portions of the Island, but chiefly West Brighton, abounds with novelties that appeal to the purse. Horse-racing, minstrelsy, dancing, necromancy, "merry-go-rounds," "Aunt Sally," weighing machines, lung testers, strength testers, swings, photograph tents, dime museums and side shows, acrobatic feats, pistol and rifle shooting, donkey and pony riding on the beach, the "Elephant" "Punch and Judy," etc., etc.

In fact nearly every comfort, luxury and amusement for the enjoyment of man, woman and child, can be found at the Island. No city in Europe can rival New York in the possession of so magnificent a stretch of beach, lying, as it does, at our very doors. Probably no other resort in the world has so many attractions to meet the public fancy; and certainly no seaside spot is so well appreciated and so largely patronized.

MANHATTAN BEACH

lies at the eastern end of the Island, and is chiefly patronized by the élite of New York city and Brooklyn who choose to favor Coney Island with their presence. A greater capital is probably here invested—under one corporation—than in any other watering place upon the Atlantic coast. The property of the Manhattan Beach Company embraces the Oriental and Manhattan hotels, the picnic and bathing pavilions, and the Firework's Park.

The Oriental hotel is that large and beautiful structure furthest east, as complete in all its parts as it is possible to build a hotel in this age of improvement and invention. It is 6 and 7 stories high, 478 feet long, and ornamented with 8 large circular towers rising 40 feet above the roof, each surmounted by a minaret 15 feet high. There are 480 sleeping rooms, furnished in elegant style, and the character of its guests are of the exclusive class. Quiet and refinement are its prevailing characteristics, and though a most delightful retreat for its guests, the general public find little to draw them to its grounds, save the magnitude and beauty of its surroundings.

The Manhattan Beach hotel, the grounds of which adjoin those of the Oriental to the westward, is the centre of attraction for the select crowd of visitors that flock hither daily, and is the especial delight of the opulent and hightoned New Yorker. The hotel is a wooden structure ornate in design, 660 feet long, and 3 and 4 stories in hight, the largest of its kind in the world. It is furnished with Eastlake furniture and superbly appointed throughout. The permanent guests occupy the upper floors, transient guests the broad piazzas and the lower floor. In its arrangements and management it is well calculated for the entertainment of the public and the comfort and pleasure of its patrons. The restaurant is served a la carte. Four thousand people can dine at one time, and 30,000 during the day. In a grand pavilion near the hotel 1,500 persons can sit at table. Visitors who bring their own luncheon are provided for here, and capital dinners of sea-food can be had. During the sultry days of midsummer many thousands refresh the inner man at the restaurant and bar; and upon the roomy balcony running along the entire façade of the building, the

ORIENTAL HOTEL.

social little coteries to be seen partaking of Manhattan's good cheer—"otum cum dignitate," as is always the rule here—would disarrange the equipoise of the most bilious temperament. The "swells" and "nabobs" of European aristocracy favor Manhattan, and a stray duke, earl, marquis or possibly a prince, may be found hovering around incog.

The railroad depot is at the rear of the hotel, a marine railway runs westward along the shore to the Brighton Beach hotel, and eastward to the boating and fishing pavilion at Point Breeze. The Music Stand, encircled by settees, is directly in front of the hotel, where the public are invited to enjoy the afternoon and evening concerts.

The Bathing Pavilion to the left comprise 2,700 separate rooms, and its appointments are perfect in every respect. The beach in front is fenced in, and the enclosed space rigidly reserved for bathers. Large floats beyond the breakers afford resting and diving places for expert swimmers, and life-boats patrol the beach at the same point. The Ladies' bathing houses are separate, and hot and cold salt-water baths in private rooms are provided for those who do not like surf bathing. In the Fireworks enclosure brilliant pyrotechnical displays are given at stated intervals.

* * *

BRIGHTON BEACH.

This famous resort lies contiguous to Manhattan Beach, and possesses many qualities that have given Manhattan so great a reputation. Somewhat more cosmopolitan however in its character, there is a free-and-easy going style among its patrons that makes strangers at home the moment they step upon its domain. It is a favorite trysting place for prominent men of all professions.

The Brighton Beach hotel is a splendid ornamental wooden structure, 525 feet long and three stories high, with broad piazzas extending its whole length. From its various towers unlimited bunting streams, as it does in fact with holiday gaiety from every building on the beach. The upper floors are reserved for permanent guests, and transient visitors are not permitted to ascend the stairways. The balcony on the second floor has 168 rooms opening on it, and meals are furnished on the table-d'hote plan. The first floor and balconies are devoted to transient guests The hotel is finished in hard wood, furnished with Eastlake furniture and Axminster carpets, and gas, running water, and ample closets, are among the conveniences provided. Two thousand persons can be seated at the tables on the balconies and in the dining-rooms at one time, and 20,000 persons can be fed during the day.

In front of the hotel the grounds are laid out with walks and grass and flowers, a little the worse for the strong salt air. The ocean made serious inroades at this spot the past winter. The Brighton Beach Race Course is situated back of the hotel, and during the racing season is well patronized by the votaries of the turf. Many exciting contests between the best horses of the land take place here, whereat the bookmakers drive a flourishing trade. Nearly every day during the season there are races at this place, or at Coney Island Race Course, which lies a short distance further east toward Sheepshead Bay.

There are two modes of transit between Brighton and West Brighton beaches : an elevated railroad starting from the Brighton hotel, going back of the Concourse, and ending at Paul Bauer's—the round trip 5 cents ; a stage line along Surf Avenue. This boulevard is a pleasant stroll for pedestrians—the distance between the two beaches is not very great—over the concrete walk on the ocean side of the drive.

Leaving Brighton Beach hotel for West Brighton, you approach a large structure to the right of the road. This is the Ocean hotel, to which is attached a bathing pavilion. About midway on the right the Grand Central hotel marks the junction of the Ocean Park Way and Surf Avenue. On the Concourse opposite the Park Way a summer house affords promenaders a chance to rest. Here one may sit as long as he pleases, sheltered from the summer sun, and fanned by the breeze wafted across the sparkling surface of the great Atlantic. Near by, the once popular Coney Island Road joins the boulevard, and now forms the terminus of the horse railroad from Brooklyn. Several hotels cluster about this old spot, notably the Grand Union hotel. This house has a commanding and unobstructed view of the sea. A short distance back, in a clump of trees, stands a relic of the past—Thompson's hotel. At the junction of this road and the boulevard is Vanderveer's hotel and stables.

WEST BRIGHTON BEACH

is about a mile west of Brighton Beach, and is to the democratic masses the real Coney Island. Distinction of class or person never has nor never will be tolerated here ; but in the good old democratic fashion, "you pays your money and you has your choice." No matter how fanciful you may be there is variety enough to choose from ; in fact one is fairly bewildered by the multiplicity of inducements offered for his mental and physical entertainment.

A pier 1000 feet long, constructed of tubular iron piles, runs out from West Brighton. On it are three two-story structures of great size containing saloons and a promenade. There are also 1,200 bath rooms, and stairways leading down into the water beneath the pier. Steamboats from New York land hourly. Near it is another pier of equal size known as the "Old" Iron Pier (at which boats also land regularly). It is opposite to the building in which the Exposition is held. The latter is commonly known as the Sea Beach Palace, and is a spacious iron and glass structure about 400 feet long by 360 feet deep. It was originally erected at the expense of the United States Government at the Centennial Exposition in Philadelphia, at a cost exceeding $100,000. At the close of the Exhibition it was purchased at auction where it stood by Messrs. Murphy & McCormack, perhaps the largest property owners in the town of New Utrecht, and who were the original projectors and promoters of the Sea Beach Railroad.

This railroad is justly called the "air line" from New York to Coney Island. Its boats leave the foot of Whitehall street, terminus of the Elevated railroads, at frequent intervals during the entire year, and during the months of June, July and August running as often as at twenty-minute intervals. Passengers are landed by the boats after a fifteen minutes' sail, upon the spacious pier at Bay Ridge, from whence over a double track route six miles in length they are conveyed with great rapidity directly southward to the centre of West Brighton, Coney Island. It is but a just tribute to the company to say that in spite of the enormous crowds which have visited Coney Island for years by means of its boats and trains, there has never been an accident of any description, nor the life of a passenger lost, nor has there

SEA BEACH PALACE HOTEL.

ever been a serious delay caused by the failure of the company to provide means of transportation to the thousands of passengers daily seeking the Island by this most popular route.

The railroad is lined on either side by fragrant market gardens in a high state of cultivation, the country seats of wealthy gentlemen, and, as it approaches Coney Island, by salt marshes closely resembling those of the low countries of Europe. To the trained eye of one who has made a study of the beauties of nature, the winding creeks and flat green meadows, flooded at high-tide, and yielding to the atmosphere a perfume of their own, grant a positive relief from the reeking air of the cities, and a most agreeable transitive stage between the inland zephyrs of New Utrecht and the sharp, salt breezes of the beach.

The trains after traversing Gravesend, the oldest English settlement of Western Long Island, founded in the early part of the 17th century by Lady Deborah Moody (who was with her household massacred by the Indians), and after skirting the shores of Gravesend Bay, affording in the distance a pleasant vista of the green shores of Staten Island, and Forts Hamilton, Lafayette and Wadsworth (which guard the entrance to New York from foreign invasion), deliver their passengers in the spacious depot which we have already described.

The schedule time by this route from Whitehall street, New York, to Coney Island, is thirty-seven minutes, and in this connection it is rather a singular fact that if two persons simultaneously leave the City Hall in New York and the City Hall in Brooklyn, and the one leaving New York goes to Coney Island by the Sea Beach Route, he will reach there at least five minutes in advance of the person starting from the City Hall in Brooklyn, no matter what route the latter may take.

The railroad owns at the Coney Island terminus a large tract of property which it is rapidly rendering more and more attractive as a popular resort. A broad avenue to the sea, shortly to be lined with shade trees, stretches from the central or main entrance of the terminal depot to the beach (a distance of about 800 feet), by means which the public may rapidly and pleasantly pass to the water's edge.

In the terminal building is now located the permanent summer exposition of machinery and the industrial arts, established and maintained under the auspices of the railroad company, and of which a brief notice may not be uninteresting. Holders of tickets over this road are admitted without charge, while all others pay a small admission fee. When it is considered that from five thousand to thirty thousand passengers per day are landed in the building throughout the summer season by the Sea beach railroad alone the value of the Exposition as an advertising medium may seem to be great. But in addition to this number must be taken into consideration the persons landed at the iron piers by the iron steamboats (from New York, Newark and other points) within a stone's throw of the Exposition building; the immense Brooklyn contingent delivered directly at the west end of the Exposition building by the Brooklyn, Bath and West End railroad; the enormous number of passengers brought to the Island by the Manhattan and Brighton railroads (who traverse Coney Island from east to west to visit the Exposition and other attractions of West Brighton), and the almost equally large contribution of the Prospect Park and Coney Island railroad, and the Coney Island and Brooklyn horse car railroad landed but a thousand feet to the east of the Sea Beach Palace.

In the Exposition building itself many things are worthy of notice. Perhaps the most interesting feature is the 125-horse power Corliss engine exhibited by Messrs. Hewes & Phillips, of Newark, which operates in part the electric light plant of the company and the numerous machinery exhibits scattered through the building. Among the latter may be mentioned that of the Fort Wayne-Jenney Electric Light Company, occupying a floor space about forty feet square, by which the major part of the lights used in Coney Island are generated. Another interesting exhibit is that of McChesney, the famous Mohawk wood-sawyer, whose wonderful sleight of hand enables him to turn out in a moment artistic objects of every description, from peg-tops to pianos. Adjoining this is Mitchell's silk loom, by which, in the twinkling of an eye, handkerchiefs containing an embroidered representation of the Exposition building are manufactured in the presence of the purchaser. Another machine near by devours an ordinary board and delivers on the other side complete cigars boxes, even to the imprint of the manufacturer and the Custom House stamp. An enterprising Shoe-black-

ing firm exhibit an old mill with water wheel in motion and
a number of live alligators disporting themselves in a tank
of liquid blacking, intended, no doubt to demonstrate the
harmless qualities of the mixture when applied upon leather,
whether made from the hide of reptiles or of mammals. An
individual dubbing himself "Paper King" has erected for
himself a veritable palace of paper from the throne of which
he holds forth the virtues of his art to admiring multitudes.
Here, too, such firms as Wechsler & Abraham, the largest
retail fancy goods house of Brooklyn, have erected in red
and white napkins a fac simile of their establishment in
Fulton street ; and F. W. Devoe & Co., the largest wholesale
paint house in New York, have placed a characteristic exhibit.
Glass blowing in all its forms may be seen, and a thousand
and one novelties varying from day to day afford amusement
over and over again to the patrons of the road. Concerts
are given day and evening by a band of picturesque mando-
line players calling themselves the Venetian Troubadours.
But it is idle to attempt discussion in detail of the numerous
features of the Exposition. They must be seen to be appreciated, and we must refer the reader to the official catalogue.

Perhaps the most useful information however is in regard
to the hotel and restaurant of Major Butler, whose experience
during the last twenty years as proprietor of the Mansion
House at Long Branch entitles him perhaps to the foremost
place among the hotel keepers of Coney Island. The hotel
contains accommodations for some 300 guests and is run,
contrary to the general principle of the Island, upon the
European plan, and at rates even less onerous than those of
hotels of the same class in the city of New York. Its rooms
have a reputation for comfort second to none, and have been
newly furnished and carpeted for the present season.

Adjoining the Exposition on the east as the Elephant ad-
joins it on the west, is the Cyclorama "Battle of Tebean,"
which connoisseurs have pronounced to be artistically the
finest of all the works of art of this description. There is
no exaggeration in this. The picture is 400 feet in length
(arranged in a circle) and 50 feet in height, and well repays
a visit. The price of admission to the general public is 25
cents. Passengers of the Sea Beach railroad however are by
exclusive contract admitted on production of their return
tickets at 15 cents each.

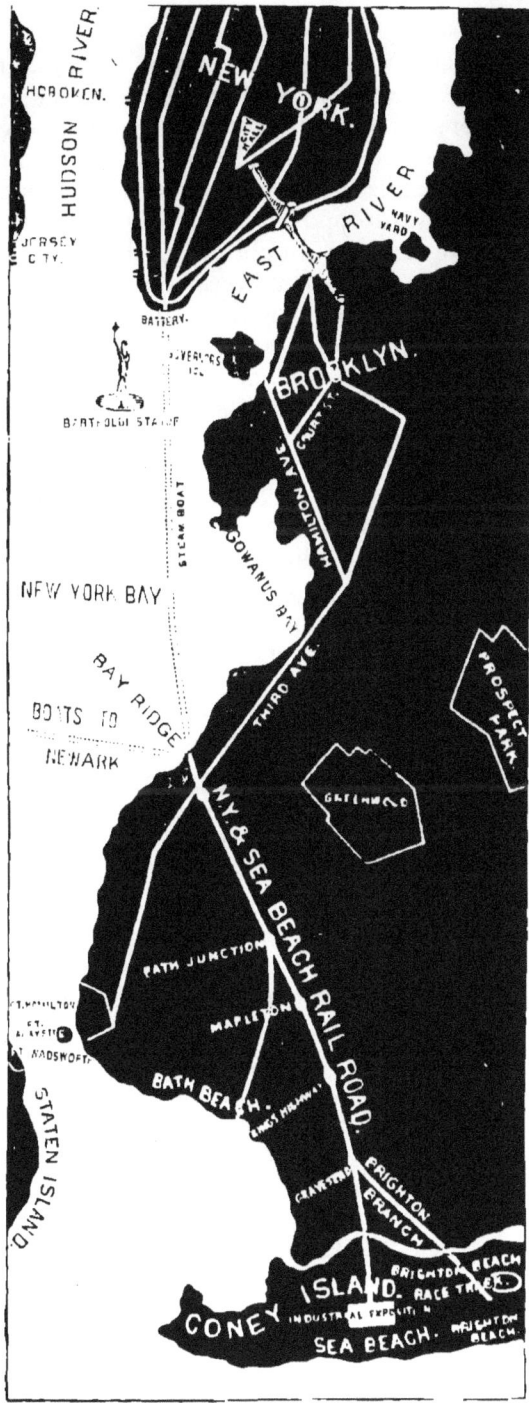

Map of the SEA BEACH ROUTE

To CONEY ISLAND. WEST BRIGHTON AND BRIGHTON BEACH RACE COURSE.

It may be useful to the general visitor to know that if his means are limited, and the prices of meals in Major Butler's or Paul Bauer's pretentious establishments are beyond his purse, meals of excellent quality and at exceedingly low prices can be procured at the "Smithonian" Restaurant on Sea Beach Boulevard opposite Feltman's Pavilion.

To the stranger West Brighton Beach is suggestive of a great fair ground. There is a breezy exhilaration in the air that braces up the most languid visitor. The music, the gay bunting flying in the breeze, the confused hum of a vast multitude of pleasure-seekers, all make up a scene not soon to be forgotten. The most conspicuous object on the Island is the Colossal Elephant at West Brighton, directly at the terminus of the Sea Beach Railroad. It is an unique and wonderful structure, and rivits the attention at once. It ought to be a source of pride to the mind that conceived it, and redounds to the credit of the Company that had the energy and the enterprise to enter upon and to carry to completion so gigantic an undertaking. It is appropriately named by its courteous and progressive manager, the Eighth Wonder of the World. It is erected on one of the most eligible and centrally located sites on the Island. It is surrounded by spaceous and tastefully-fitted up grounds, where visitors may take their lunch —tables and all necessary conveniences being provided gratuitously to them by the proprietors of this most popular resort. Concerts are given in one of the rooms of the Elephant. That the reader may form some idea of the magnitude of this mammoth structure the writer will give a detailed statement of its proportions. Its height is 175 feet, 6 inches; its length is 203 feet; length of body 109 feet; inside circumference 198 feet; length of neck 19 feet; circumference of neck 128 feet; length of legs 60 feet; circumference of legs 80 feet; length of ears 54 feet; width of ears 40 feet: length of tail 70 feet; diameter of tail 18 feet, tapering to 26 inches: diameter of trunk 20 feet; length of trunk 72 feet; length of tusks 42 feet, diameter 12 feet tapering to one inch. The eyes, which are composed of glass 2 inches thick, are 4 feet in diameter. The gallery is 298 feet long, extending from the body 15 feet around the main hall on the inside. The canopied saddle or "howdah" is 38 feet square and 42 feet high, from which a magnificent view can be had for 50 miles around of the Bay of New York,

ELEPHANTINE COLOSSUS, WEST BRIGHTON, CONEY ISLAND.

the ocean, the City, etc. The Elephant is divided into 31
rooms : a main hall head room, 2 side body rooms, 2 thigh
rooms, 2 shoulder rooms, 2 cheek rooms, 1 throat room, 1
stomach room, 4 hoof rooms, 6 leg rooms, 2 side rooms, 2
hip rooms, 1 through room from which the Elephant is feed-
ing. Perfect ventilation is secured through the medium of
63 windows, and at night the entire structure is brilliantly
illuminated by 25 electric lights, which are equal to 175,000
candles. The Elephant in its construction consumed about
3,500,000 feet of lumber, 11,000 kegs of nails, 12 tons of
iron bolts, and it is covered by 57,000 square feet of tin.
It can all be taken apart and transferred on pealing off the
tin. It took 263 men 120 full working days to build it,
and was dedicated August, 1884. The entire cost of the
work was nearly a quarter of a million of dollars. This
wonderful curiosity is located on Surf Avenue, the principal
thoroughfare on the Island, and adjoining the Sea Beach
Palace. It also faces the ocean, and the twin iron piers.
It stands close by the terminus of most all of the different
railroads and steamboats, the horse car lines, and main drives
from Brooklyn to Coney Island. J. T. McCaddon Esq. is
the manager of this gigantic marvel, and Henry Sweatman
the advertising press agent. The price of admission is 10
cents. The season commenced on Decoration Day. Prys-
matic fountains, and elegant sward add their attractions to
the place. One side of the grounds is lined with cafes and
lunch rooms. The area altogether occupied by this exhibition is much larger than that taken up by any other single
enterprise on the Island. Scarcely a person visits the Island
who does not go to see the Elephant. The contractor
agreed that this structure should last 50 years. Its founda-
tion is laid 30 feet under the ground

Next to the Elephant the most noticeable object at West
Brighton is the Observatory, towering 300 feet toward the
sky, and from the top, reached by elevators, a fine view of
the Island, the bay, and the adjacent cities may be obtained.

Close by the observatory will be seen the Great Natural
Curiosity—" a live cow stuffed with straw," as we once over-
heard a " jokist" call it—that yields 100 gallons of ice cold
milk a day, and more, if necessity demands it; milk pure
and sweet, like the pretty dairy maids that serve the custo-
mers at a nickle per glass.

They that chose to ignore the lacteal fluid for something of more pungent taste, will find the dairy flanked on the left by the mill, where sweet cider, " fresh from the press," is sold by the glass. For something stronger yet drop in on Mr. Frash, the widely known and popular wine merchant, of No. 10 Barclay street, New York city, who is proprietor of one of the most attractive and inviting pavilions at this most charming sea-side resort. His cosy retreat is eligibly located between the Iron Piers and near the palatial hotel of Paul Bauer. Mr. Flash makes a specialty of Champagne, and sells none but the purest and best. The conveniences, comforts and luxuries of this pavilion, which was founded by this gentleman some eight years since, makes his establishment a most pleasant place of resort to those wishing to indulge in a glass or bottle of American Champagne. Here the thirsty visitor may procure those delicious and palatable wines of the Pacific slope, and enjoy the sparkling beverage amid the most charming surroundings, and in quantities that cannot fail to satisfy his desires in the melting summer days. Some idea may be formed of the extent of business transacted when the reader is informed that it is no unusual occurrance for him to open five hundred bottles a day during the heated term.

Pie, cake and bon-bon merchants are numerous, and at booths laden with confections the " sweet tooth" is provided for. The fried Frankfurt sausage man is at all times ready with his savory dish, and there are a dozen places where a pan of succulent clams awaits your order for roasting.

That machine, like an antiquated air-pump, will tell your pulling strength ; and the one beside it, your striking force. The man with rueful visage owns the blowing machine; but such wonderful phenomena in this line has he met since he came to the Island, that he mourns the incapacity of his machine to test their powers—for ordinary mortals his apparatus is adequate to the fiercest blast. Yon silver-haired Mentor, with polished scales and dignified mien, will show your exact weight for 5 cents. Many other kindred attractions take transient quarters in this versatile place, and the cries of the pop-corn and peanut men, and itinerants of that ilk, add to the general hubbub.

A Camera Obscura here gives charming views of the beach, sharply outlined, delicately toned, and worth seeing.

On the left of the boulevard, across the broad plaza, is
Bauer's West Brighton Beach hotel, a large structure practi-
cally forming the nucleus of the buildings scattered about.
Mr. Paul Bauer was one of the pioneers in the improvements of Coney Island. In 1876 he erected the spacious
hotel just referred to, which is one of the best of its kind on
the Atlantic sea shore. Centrally and delightfully located,
midway between the two iron piers, it commands attention
of the multitudes that daily seek the kaleidescopic pleasures
of West Brighton. The hotel has 100 well furnished sleeping apartments, the restaurant and pavilion can accommo-
date many thousands, and in the turrets that adorn the
building there are elegantly furnished rooms where retired
parties can escape the throng below. It is complete and
perfect in all its appointments, with all modern improvements. The dining room is immense in extent, of unrivalled
seating capacity; the tables are handsomely furnished, and
the room is unique in all its equipments, while delightful
music is discoursed by an excellent string band, the intervals
being filled in with melody from a sweet-toned Orchestrion.
The menue comprises every variety of edible that can be
procured in our home or foreign markets ; the cuisine cannot
be excelled, for skilled cooks preside in the kitchen ; the
waiters are prompt and obliging. An elegantly fitted up bar
is always provided with the choicest imported and native
wines and liquors, natural mineral waters and the various
temperance drinks, together with the best brands of Havana
and domestic cigars. In a word here the sojourner will find
every comfort and convenience. Mr. Bauer is widely recog-
nized as a thoroughly active and sterling man of business.
He personally supervises all branches of his different lines
of business, and is indefatigable in his efforts to please and
satisfy all who favor him with their patronage. That " he
knows how to keep a hotel " is evinced by the fact that his
patrons are constantly increasing in number, creating the
necessity from time to time to extend his limits and to enlarge
his accommodations.

Paul Bauer's West Brighton Casino may be classed among
the largest structures on the Island. It is located in the rear
of the hotel and is separated from it by some considerable
space. It is 300 feet long, 170 feet broad, and has a capacity for over 10,000 persons.

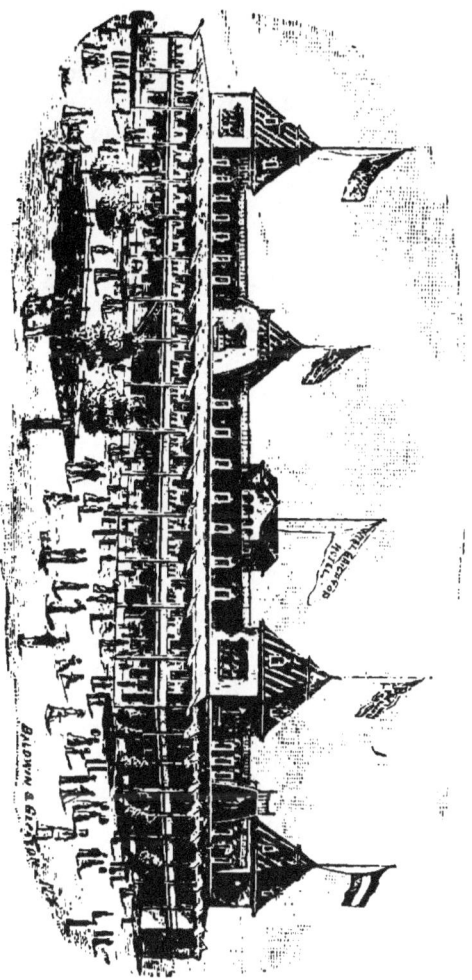

WEST BRIGHTON BEACH HOTEL.

A most novel sensation which should be classed as one of
the attractions of the Island, is that afforded by a ride on the
gravity road west of Feltman's Pavilion, and which may be
reached by passing through that huge building from the
Sea Beach Railroad.

* * *

WEST END

Comprises all that portion of the Island from West Brighton
to the extreme western end, familiar as Norton's Point. The
natural beauties of this locality are superior to any other
part of the Island. From the Point an extended view can
be had of Princess Bay, Staten Island, the Narrows, Forts
Hamilton and Wadsworth, the beautiful shores of Gravesend
Bay, Bath Beach, the Jersey Highlands, and Sandy Hook
in the distance. Capital has not invaded this district in the
same ratio as it has the rest of the Island ; hence its present
aspect partakes more of the " Old Coney Island " before
spoken of. Several quaint, old-fashioned hotels exist in
their pristine glory ; and there are many Gothamites who so
fondly cling to " auld lang syne" that no inducement could
swerve their attachment to these ancient sands.

Scattered over West End there are numbers of small
enclosures and sheds, " ycleped pavilions," furnishing light,
refections and bathing facilities, where parties that wish to
avoid the commotion betake themselves.

THE BEACH AT THE WEST END.

BATH BEACH.

BATH BEACH (formerly Bath) is a beautiful suburban village on the Long Island shore of the Narrows, about two miles below Fort Hamilton. It is one of the old Dutch settlements on Long Island, and contains a number of substantial and roomy houses of the old style.

The township covers a considerable expanse of ground, portions of it being quite level, other parts gently undulating or rolling. The streets (which are called avenues) are long and straight, and of proper width, running longitudinally and traversely to the limits of the borough, dividing it into large squares or blocks. They are embellished with trees (recently planted), which separate the roadbed from the planked sidewalks.

The facilities for bathing at this charming retreat are scarcely equalled, certainly not excelled, by any of the neighboring seaside resorts. Here you can be buffeted by the undulating and swelling waves without fear of that dangerous undertow, or the violent tossing of the foaming surge, so much of a drawback to the nervous votary of Neptune, who courts the embrace of the Atlantic at Coney Island and elsewhere. Here noisy, gleeful childhood takes its first lessons in the art of swimming; and probably one of the most entertaining sights of this delightful bay is that afforded by the antics of the young, of both sexes, gamboling upon the soft sea-washed sands, and running valiantly into the water to gleefully meet the coming wave. Verily, they seem like so many amphibious animals, creatures of both elements, and the noisy, exhilarating exercise brings to their chubby cheeks the rosy blush of the purest health.

In many of our watering places the heat of the sun deters visitors from taking out-of-door exercise except in the morning or evening. It is otherwise in Bath. The overhanging foliage of its magnificent trees protects the promenaders and the drives from the scorching rays of the sun, and permits one to go about without fear of being melted alive.

The principal thoroughfare is called Cropsy Avenue. It runs the entire length of the beach, and on the side facing the water, stand most of the hotels, backed by a high bluff reaching around the water front. A perpendicular dock is constructed along the greater part of it, from the beach to the top of the bluff, even with the surface of the street. The beach is reached by following the streets running toward and terminating at the shore, and by stairs built from parts of the hotels and boarding houses

Artificial awnings and balconies are rare nere, being uncalled for, as nature in her sylvan dress supplies the necessary protection. Under its cool arbors children can romp and gambol along the shores, while their parents look on fearless of sunstroke or other dangers incident to an exposure to the rays of a summer's sun. Bath is a woodland village set on ocean's verge.

A great source of amusement is to watch the yachts and ocean steamers sailing up and down the bay. As a variation between flag guessing and yacht racing, another speculative sport for the visitors is to bet the drinks on the Line and name of the outgoing and incoming steamers, predicating their judgment on the color of their smoke stacks as near as they can distinguish the same in the intervening distance.

Amid its multifarious attractions we should not neglect to mention that fine fishing may be enjoyed a short distance from its shores.

Beside its almost unequalled natural advantages and attractions as a summer resort, its near proximity to New York (time and space between these points being reduced to a minimum by the unsurpassed facilities for transit back and forth) has attracted as permanent summer residents to this most delightful locality, many of New York and Brooklyn's first families, best citizens and wealthiest merchants.

The following railroads run between New York City, Brooklyn and Bath Beach every 30 minutes during the summer months:

Sea Beach Railroad by steamer from foot of Whitehall street, New York, connecting with trains at Bay Ridge, and making close connection with the *Brooklyn, Bath and West End Railroad* at Bath Junction.

Brooklyn, Bath and West End Railroad from Greenwood Cemetery, Brooklyn, passing through Bath to Coney Island every 20 minutes.

There are also two steamboats plying between New York and Bath Beach every 30 minutes, so that the facilities to reach this attractive watering place make it the most desirable resort for the inhabitants of New York and Brooklyn during the summer months.

The hotels at Bath Beach are spacious and finely located, offering the very best accommodations at reasonable prices. The many cottage boarding houses in the village are picturesquely situated, and good rooms and excellent board can be obtained within the means of even an economical visitor.

The appreciation of real estate, in any locality, is always the best evidence of its substantial prosperity. Judged by this criterion Bath Beach stands second to none of the watering places within its vicinity. Village lots that could have been purchased a few years ago at a nominal figure have doubled and trebled, and in some instances, quadrupled in value.

FORT HAMILTON.

ONE of the most delightful of the many summer resorts in the vicinity of New York and Brooklyn is Fort Hamilton. Its location, a most charming one, is on a promontory of New York Bay, on the south-west shore of Long Island, about two miles from Bath. It is almost directly opposite Fort Wadsworth, which is built on a headland of the Staten Island shore, and forms part of a mountain rising to a great elevation as it runs back from the bay, affording from the Fort Hamilton side a grand view of a romantic, varied and picturesque country.

The growth of Fort Hamilton during the last two or three years has been phenomenal. Its increase in commercial accommodations has been commensurate with its advance in popularity and favor. There is no kind of sea-side pleasure that cannot be found here, affording to young and old and to both sexes, all the innocent recreation their hearts can desire. Croquet, base-ball, dancing on the green beneath the shade of trees, or in the pavilions, practicing in the shooting galleries, knocking down the rag babies with balls, playing at " Old Aunt Sally," trying one's skill in the bowling alleys, billiard rooms and at the shuffle boards velocipede riding, roller skating, goat and pony carriages for children, flying horses .or merry-go-rounds, swings, fortune telling and other shows too numerous to particularize. Then there are the bands of music and the vocal exhibitions by talented songsters, that even the birds in the trees might well envy. What a catalogue of enjoyment within a stone's throw, we might say, of this city. Who would not exchange the stifling atmosphere and the furnace-like streets for the

cool breeze down the bay? Who would not infinitely prefer to lay off at one's ease beneath the shady retreats along
the Narrows, than gasp for the breath of air denied us even
in our city parks? How much pleasure, at so insignificant a
cost, lies at our very door, and where is the obstacle that can
debar us from the delights of such a charming spot as Fort
Hamilton?

It is not speaking in hyperbole to state that the fishing
advantages of this place are not surpassed, if equalled, any
where within a long distance of our city. It may be almost
called the fisherman's elysium, and that its waters are highly
appreciated on this account, is shown by the many people
who are attracted to this place on fishing excursions. On a
clear, calm day, no matter how fervid may be the rays of the
sun, its waters will be thickly dotted with skiffs and boats,
every kind of small craft in fact, anchored at chosen points
on the bay, and from which the occupants cast their lines
with more or less success.

All the choice and delicate variety of fish may be caught
in this vicinity, and on days that are propitious for fishing,
you could imagine you were among men that had but one
object in life, and that object, fish; while angling for the
finny tribe, their tongues are continually on the wag, whereof
the burden of their conversation is fish, first, last and
always.

A very healthful and pleasing recreation it is to sit under
the shade of the trees on the south shore, or under the
covered porches of its hotels, inhaling the cooling breezes of
the bay, and enjoying the sight of the white sails of the ships
of all sizes, from the stately three-master, in the pride of her
strength, with all her white canvass spread, to the single sail
cat-boat; from the majestic steamer, as she puffs and plows
her way through the waters of the bay, to the many little tug
boats that snort and whistle with such vigor, after the fashion
of all little productions, both of nature and art, which are
forever trying to make a great noise in the world. The railroad from Brooklyn to Fort Hamilton runs along a
road sheltered from the rays of the sun by overarching trees,
planted on either side, affording a pleasing shelter and an
interesting view of fine fertile farm land.

Many of the farmers along this road give evidence of
prosperity, and an appreciation of the beautiful, showing

fine architectural judgment in the erection of the dwellings
and outhouses.

From a military point of view, Nature has made this one
of the most effective sites for the purposes of fortification that
the protection of our great metropolis could demand.
Seconded as this promontory is by the one directly opposite,
upon which stands Fort Wadsworth, the water approach
toward New York is here reduced to a narrow channel,
though which an investing fleet must pass before the city
will be completely under the enemy's guns. It is true that
the perfection reached by modern artillery, in longe range
effectiveness, would enable some of the iron-clads of the first
class to shell the city of New York from a point beyond
even Coney Island, and thus dispense with the necessity of
threading the channel between the forts above mentioned ;
but this is no reason why so admirable a point of defence
should be neglected, and we are glad to know that its natural advantages are appreciated.

Another pleasing sight are the soldiers in all the glory of
full uniform, marching and countermarching during certain
hours of the day, forming a perfect kaleidescopic view that
cannot fail to be of interest to even the most unmartial
spectator. And the gallant bearing of the officers, both on
foot and on horseback; what palpitating sensations do not
these noble looking men engender in the breasts of artless
and impressible females. Who shall take the palm in the
ladies' hearts from the " bould soldier boy."

The officers' quarters or residences are attractive structures,
with neatly arranged surroundings, on which, at appropriate
seasons of the year, admirable floral and horticultural taste
is displayed. The officers' families, mingling with the many
solid and conservative merchants of New York and Brooklyn. who abide here permanently during the summer
months, make a refined and pleasant society at this place
during the season.

Only a few years since it took nearly a half a day to reach
Fort Hamilton from New York or Brooklyn, the only means
of public transit being the horse cars. Now there are steam
cars running every five minutes from the horse car junction,
at 20th Street and 3d Avenue, Brooklyn.

There has been recently established a water route having
a terminus adjoining the South Ferry slip in New York. It

connects at 35th Street and 3d Avenue, Brooklyn, with the
steam cars direct to Fort Hamilton. This mode of transit
costs but five cents.

The hotel and boarding-house accommodations are very
good, the cuisine of all of them giving great satisfaction,
which is considerable to say for the average country hostelry.
The table is supplied with the varied products of the rich
farming lands in the neighborhood ; the choicest of fish
fresh from their native element, and the best that the great
markets of New York City afford ; while the prices are reasonable, and vary according to the pretentiousness of the
establishment.

One of the finest and coolest shades in the vicinity of New
York is the South Shore road leading to Bay Ridge. It is
bordered by handsome villas set amid artistically laid out
pleasure grounds. Here the overhanging majestic trees
interlace their broad foliage, and the observant spectator
will note a thousand beauties in this charming thoroughfare
where art and nature both unite to form a picture of peren-
nial beauty.

During the yachting season Bay Ridge heights are crowded
with enthusiastic spectators, many equipped with field and
opera glasses with which they sweep the Narrows and Bay
after a very nautical fashion. From this point there is a
splendid view to be obtained of every craft afloat within
sight. The brilliant costumes of the ladies lend a variety to
the picture, and the sight both on land and on water is gay
and exhilarating. Many a fair lady tosses her handkerchief
to the breeze as encouragement to some favorite boat or
oarsman, and the shouts of the men make the air ring
again.

Fort Lafayette, situated between Fort Hamilton and Fort
Wadsworth, reminds one, in its present dilapidated state, of
those ancient towers of Europe, which still look formidable
even in decay. During the late war it was used as a prison
for political offenders. A number of well-known persons
suspected of treasonable designs were arrested and confined
in this fort. It was destroyed by fire on December 1, 1868,
and the works have never been restored.

Fort Hamilton is noted for its fine cottages. The Norton
Cottage, a pleasantly situated and attractive building, stands
in the midst of tastefully laid out grounds, the portion in

the immediate vicinity of the house being a marvel of floral-culture. The cottage, interiorly considered, is large, home-like and handsomely furnished. There are 16 rooms, two of which are parlors. Mr. and Mrs. Norton have had years of experience in keeping summer boarders, and few know better how to cater in the most acceptable manner to the most fastidious. A part of the grounds is devoted to the cultivation of garden-truck, so that the table (we are told they set an excellent one) is never at a loss for the freshest of vegetables ; and as for butter and fresh milk there are the sleek looking cows to answer for that.

Perhaps there is not in the village a larger and more sub-stantial building than the residence of Mrs. H. H. Clapp. It is conspicuously and pleasantly located, near and in full view of the most elegant hotel of the village, and command-ing a grand prospect of the ocean, and from its upper windows of a wide stretch of surrounding country. The house is built in the midst of wide surrounding grounds, thickly studded with trees of many year's growth, the large spreading branches affording the finest shade imaginable. The parlors are elegantly furnished, and the sleeping rooms models of comfort and convenience. Its site is most conve-nient, being situated on the corner of Shore Road and Third Avenue, scarcely more than a minute's walk from the Grand View Hotel, and hence it is easy for the lodgers of the house to take their meals at that elegant hostelry. It is not the purpose of Mrs. Clapp (a most estimable lady, by the way) to take table boarders, except under special circumstances.

Mr. Charles P. Cole, the enterprising photographer, has six photographic galleries—four on Coney Island and two at Fort Hamilton. At the former place two of his art studios are alongside of the new iron pier, and the other two on what is known as the Vanderbilt property. At Fort Hamilton one is situated on the property connected with the Sea View hotel, kept by Mr. John Napier ; the other opposite the United States hotel. A fine view is had from the latter of the Narrows, protected on either side by Forts Richmond, Wadsworth and Hamilton. Any one desiring a good picture should not fail to pay this artist a visit, either here or at Coney Island. Mr. Cole was the first to establish a photo-graphic studio at Fort Hamilton ; while he is the longest established man in the business on the Island.

The United States, so ably conducted by Mr. Michael Gates, is situated on that elevated plateau where the visitor to Fort Hamilton is landed on leaving the cars at Brooklin R. R. depot. This hostelry commands a fine view of the Narrows, and takes in both the upper and lower bays. Stairs lead down to the water's edge where boating facilities are always to be had, and where, if you desire it, you can be equipped with fishing tackle and bait. Mr. Gates and his brother are both practical and experienced fishermen, ready at any time to cater to the wants of patrons bent on a fishing excursion. Mr. Gates though not keeping lodgers can find accommodations for permanent visitors in neighboring houses. A restaurant is connected with the house, and the proprietor gives table board by the week, or meals a la carte.

Mr. Gustave Beierlein will this year add greatly to the attractiveness of his summer pavilion. A new building has been erected with a balcony frontage of 120 feet and depth of 75 feet, from which visitors, while partaking of refreshments, may enjoy the bracing salt air, and take in at the same time a fine ocean and coast view. On the left can be seen Bath and Coney Island; in the distance Rockaway; to the right Staten Island and the stubborn elevations of the Highlands of Neversink; and looking seaward may be seen the incoming and outgoing steamers and sailing vessels—in fact every description of water craft. The tables are supplied with all the delicacies of the market, while the choicest wines, liquors and cigars are to be had at the bar. Music is furnished by a full orchestra.

A notable instance of the growth of Fort Hamilton in four years is the popular Hostelrie established in this place by Mr. John Nappier, known as "The Sea View Hotel." Prior to its purchase by its present proprietor, it was a dairy house where the few thirsty visitors who meandered that way could slake their thirst with a glass of milk. Now the extent and variety of the refreshments is such as to satisfy the palates of all the varied classes of visitors who partake of them under his comfortable balconies, while inhaling the refreshing breezes of the Bay. Mr. Nappier has shown his good judgment in selecting this spot for his establishment, and is rewarded by the patronage of large numbers, who are as well pleased with his jovial and affable manner, as with his hospitality, which is proverbial.

SHEEPSHEAD BAY.

SHEEPSHEAD BAY is a village about two miles north-east of Coney Island, on the bay from which it is named. There are cottages and boarding-houses for summer residents, and a race course. The latter is famous in the sporting world. It is under the management of the Coney Island Jockey Club, organized in 1879, which has a fine club house at Manhattan Beach. The course has a mile track with a handsome facade at the entrance, a commodious grand stand, judges' stand, and other buildings in the Queen Anne style, erected in 1880. Race meetings, held in June and September, are very largely attended, and the results are immediately telegraphed far and wide.

It is only of late years that Sheepshead Bay has achieved notoriety as a summer resort, and a very quaint and charming little spot it is, too. Where once a few sequestered houses were scattered along the shore looking extremely miserable in their loneliness, and grateful, indeed, to be dignified as a village, now there is a continuous section of the loveliest of white cottages imaginable, including a very nice hotel, furnished with all the modern improvements. The villas are remarkable for their tasteful style of architecture and their pleasant grounds. Quite a pleasant feature at night is the congregation of the guests on the different balconies, enjoying the cool air off the bay, and planning some anticipated excursion for the following day.

Sheepshead Bay is within easy reach of the ocean. It is connected with Manhattan Beach by a bridge spanning the bay, and during the summer months this bridge is almost constantly occupied by promenaders, more especially in the

mornings and evenings. During the early part of the fore
noon, the sojourners at the village cross over in order to
enjoy an invigorating bath in the Atlantic, or to watch
others frolic in the surf, returning before the day is too far
advanced to render walking "a toil of pleasure." There are
many deliciously cool retreats at Sheepshead Bay where
visitors may retire when the sun shall have become unpleas-
antly hot; and people of a social disposition need not fear
that time will hang heavily on their hands. Then, when the
shades of evening begin to steal over the face of nature, when
the jingle of glasses and the rattle of china betokens that the
last meal of the day is over, how delightful to take one's wife
or sweetheart under your wing and saunter off down to the
bridge. The cool air off the water plays caressingly through
your hair, and sets the pretty face at your side all aglow,
until you really wonder if there is another woman in the wide
world half so charming. Perhaps the moon is just rising in
a sky cloudless and bespangled with stars, and its light tips
the waters rolling softly beneath you with a radiant pathway
of silver; and then you hear in the far distance the faint
strains of a martial air which Gilmore's famous band is just
performing. As you advance the music grows louder and
more inspiring, and finally bursting on your ear in one
triumphant blast, dies away in silence as the tune is ended.
You are now on the beach. Before you is the grand old
ocean, which has endured for ages, and will yet continue
when you are gone and forgotten of the world. It stretches
away in dim uncertain lines, lapping the shore with a gentle
swell that tells of a fine night and a calm sea.

Shall you stroll along the beach, or sit and listen to
Gilmore, or go to the fireworks, or will you combine the
three? Thus you have all the pleasures of the seashore at
your disposal while rusticating in one of the most charming
little country towns in the near vicinity of New York.

ESPLANADE

ROCKAWAY BEACH.

NEXT to Coney Island the most popular and most frequented of sea-side resorts on the Long Island shore is
that of Rockaway Beach. It is a narrow strip of land sepa-
rating Jamaica Bay from the Atlantic Ocean, and distant
about twenty miles from New York.

We know of no more pleasant trip down the Bay and out
upon the broad bosom of the sparkling sea than that afforded
by one of the Rockaway steamers on a warm summer's afternoon. Two or three of the largest excursion boats in the
world run on this route, and the fare for the round trip is but
fifty cents.

To enjoy the sail to the utmost one must board the
steamer at the starting point foot of east 34th Street, New
York. Be on hand early to avoid the last rush which generally comes at the moment of departure. Once afloat you
are treated to a magnificent panoramic display of the piers,
shipping and public buildings of the great metropolis. On
the other hand the green and sloping shores of New Jersey
shine resplendent in the sun, till Jersey City, with its piers
and ferry houses, its railroad depots, its buildings and spires,
bursts into view, and melts away finally to the south-west in
the flats and marshes for which New Jersey is celebrated.

The different piers on the New York side at which the
Rockaway boat pulls up are usually black with perspiring
excursionists, who hail the rumble of the gang-plank with a
sigh of relief. A motley assemblage, truly, in which women
and children preponderate, except perhaps of a Sunday. A
band of music on board plays popular airs, and as the boat
swings off from her berth, and your cheek is fanned by the

gentle current of air fresh from the blue scintillating ocean outside the Narrows, but which as yet you cannot see, the effect upon your senses is one of great exhilaration.

A better idea of the Harbor can be obtained by taking this trip than in any other way. After leaving the Battery, with its quaint, circular landmark (where emigrants from Europe are landed every week by the thousand from the barges which transport them from the ocean steamships), you pass Governor's Island and obtain a view of Castle William and its other defenses. Next you will observe, from the other side of the steamer, the famous Statue of Liberty, erected on Bedloe's Island. The great torch, piercing the blue ether 300 feet or more above the sea level, was placed there as significant of the enlightenment which illumines this land of glorious freedom and equality, and like a beacon pointing out to the oppressed of all nations a harbor of refuge from monarchial tyranny. Again to the left you glide by the green shores of Bay Ridge, where the pier and depot of the Manhattan Beach Railway are located; thence down through the Narrows where frown the gray walls of Fort Hamilton on the left side and Fort Wadsworth on the other, and above the latter the emerald tinted walls of the earthworks called Fort Tompkins; so on past the empty port-holes of that historical ruin yclept Fort Lafayette, and out into the lower bay. Over to the right stretches the low line of Sandy Hook, and beyond the deep blue expanse of the Atlantic glinting in the sunlight.

Coney Island presently comes in sight on the left, and then, the boat having doubled Norton's Point, where the shelving beach of white sand gleams so alluringly, you pass successively Sea Beach, with its monster elephant; West Brighton, with its two iron piers; Brighton Beach and Manhattan Beach.

Now the boat for the first time feels the swell, be it ever so slight, which is always present on the surface of the ocean. You are fairly launched upon the Atlantic, albeit you are close inshore, with the airy pavillions and gorgeous but flimsy structures of an Arabian night's enchantment spread out on your left, where a few years ago was but a waste of sand, charily visited even during the summer by our metropolitan pleasure seekers, and only then by those who came to fish or to enjoy a cool plunge in the surf, or both.

From this point the steamer hauls out, and passing through the channel in the Coney Island bar, on which the surf breaks heavily with an ever monotonous roar, and running in near Barren Island puts into Jamaica Bay and lands its passengers at one or all of the four piers on the inside of Rockaway Beach.

Landing at the first pier the excursionist, to reach the ocean side of the beach, has but to cross a broad wooden pavement under the shadow of that gigantic failure, the mammoth Rockaway hotel, erected by the Rockaway Beach Improvement Company, and which, owing to financial embarrassment, has never yet been regularly opened to the public. The general features of the beach are the same at all four landings. Unsubstantial and fantastic wooden pavillions, for dancing, drinking beer, and eating clams, abound on every hand. The dancing platforms are always in request, and the scraping of the fiddle and the pounding of pianos, rendered asthmatic by the sea air, mingle incessantly with the roar of the surf. Life lines extend into the water at intervals, and hundreds of people in uncouth bathing-dresses are rolling, tumbling and screaming with delight in the embrace of the surf. The beach is about eight miles long, but the buildings are clustered in a space of about three miles.

Beside the landings which project into Jamaica Bay there has lately been built by the Rockaway Beach Pier Company, on the ocean side, an iron pier 1,200 feet long and 30 feet wide, except at the outer extremity, where for 100 feet it is expanded to 80 feet. This section is protected by a wooden fender piling, making a triangle as a landing place for steamboats.

At the eastern end, where the beach joins the mainland, is the village of Far Rockaway, with several good summer hotels where good board can be had at very reasonable rates. There is also a sanitarium (under the auspices of St. John's Guild) at this point, where sick children are provided by charity with a week's seaside pleasure.

All the diversions of a seaside resort are to be found at Rockaway; there is certainly no lack of enticements to draw forth even the reluctant penny. And why not? One goes to the seaside to be amused; and certainly you do not expect to get it "free, gratis and for nothing."

FAR ROCKAWAY.

TO those who appreciate the substantial benefits to be derived from a sea-side resort, and who sojourn there for the purpose of improving their health and increasing their physical vigor, rather than for the mere pursuit of pleasure, there are none of the many watering places in the near vicinity of New York and Brooklyn that present greater attractions than Far Rockaway.

Situated on a high plane, facing a narrow inlet of the ocean, it commands a delightful view of fine, varied and picturesque scenery, affording attractions rivalling those of the Catskills, combined with the refreshing coolness of the sea breezes, still water bathing (which is absolutely safe), and the healthful exercise of rowing, as well as the enticing amusement of fishing, which may be here indulged in by children and women without fear of danger.

Its waters being an arm of the Atlantic, render it a safe retreat for those who are too unskilled in aquatic science to enjoy a sail on old ocean's turbulent billows. Here they can be wafted in a kell, with all its sails spread, over the placid waters of the inlet, watching the changeful tint of the water, and the ever varying shadows cast by the adjacent shores. What a delightful recreation upon a summer afternoon; the cool breezes from the sea tempering the heat, and warding off that feeling of lassitude which is attendant upon the dog days. Jamaica Bay, a little to the westward, offers the same advantages on a still larger scale.

Those who prefer a heavy surf, can enjoy it to their hearts content by crossing the narrow inlet, where they will find a reef of sand affording the best natural facilities for this more vigorous kind of bathing. Many who formerly believed that only mountain air could meet their particular need, find the exchange to this elevated sea side resort most healthful and invigorating.

Pure limpid water, free from all deleterious substances; shaded walks and pleasant drives over fine roads, flanked on either side with fertile productive fields, and winding through a picturesque country; quiet evenings on the piazzas and lawns, with freedom from mosquitoes and all unpleasant odors, are some of the many natural attractions of this place.

Its near proximity to New York and Brooklyn, both by land and water, make it one of the most desirable and convenient places of summer resort for merchants, clerks and others employed all day long in the sweltering heat of the two great cities. Here they may enjoy a few hours of grateful repose, deriving fresh vigor for next day's toil.

The hotel accommodations are varied and excellent, equipped and conducted in such various degrees of style, and both such accommodating scales of prices, as to satisfy the tastes and requirements of all classes of its sojourners, and the capacity of all purses.

The permanent summer habitues of this place are largely made up of the sensible and substantial merchants, who disdain to yield to the caprices and follies of fashion, or ape the manners of the tilted foreigners, who are allured to this place by its many natural changes and attractions over those of their native countries.

NEW YORK CITY.

On the night of November 2d last year, at the closing ceremonies attending the unveiling of that fair maid—the Goddess of Liberty—there was the most magnificent, brilliant and most gorgeous display of fireworks it has ever been the writer's privilege to behold. Even the elements lent their aid ; the heavens marshalling their batallions of inky clouds into a pall of blackness as a background to the coming fire. The Battery and its surroundings were alive with expectant and enthusiastic humanity most eager for the fray. Language is too tame and inadequate to picture to others, or to give those who could not attend the faintest conception of the brilliancy and beauty of that delightful spectacle— The magnitude and profusion of the supply ; the unusual splendor and variety of the colors ; the multitudinous and novelty of designs of the various pyrotechnical pieces, and the rapidity with which they were evolved produced a continuous illumination of many colored fires, lasting from early eve to midnight. The ever-recurring and momentary discharge of a sea of rockets, with their long and flaming tails bursting into fiery rainbows, filled the eye space with a picture no mortal can forget. Another feature of this grand display was that at short intervals baloons representing our own and the tri-colored ensign of France were sent up, belching forth, as they ascended and floated in theair, brilliantly colored milky-ways of fire sailing upward and onward till piercing the clouds like the starry harbingers of night they floated on and on into the mysteries of the heavens, leaving our imagination fired with the memory of a pyrotechnic picture undreamt of and indescribable.

This exhibition was under the personal contract and supervision of the Unexcelled Fireworks Co., 7 Park Place, New York.

Prominent in the Artists' Material line is the firm of J. Marsching & Co., 27 Park Place, corner of Church st., New York. Their stock of these goods is very complete, comprising every requisite of the student or finished artist, and purchasers would do well to call upon them. They have just published a complete illustrated catalogue which will be mailed to any address upon application. In addition to their line of Artists' Supplies, Messrs. J. Marsching & Co. carry a large stock of Bronze Powders, Gold, Silver and Metal Leaf ; also a full line of all material for Glass and China Decorating.

—   • •   —

BROOKLYN.

Among the well known business men of Brooklyn, there are none can excel in enterprise and knowledge the enterprising firm of A. M. Stein & Co., proprietors of the Excelsior Sale and Exchange Stables at 225 and 231 Washington street. The brothers Stein are professors in horse-flesh, and in their stables can always be found the finest blooded stock of this country. Their motto is square dealing, and their best advertisement is that they never lose a customer, for when he once has a transaction with them he is sure to come again. They always keep a nice selected stock of Road and Working Horses on hand which they sell or exchange. They are good citizens and honorable men.

"The Finest," 142 Flatbush av. and 661 Pacific street, Brooklyn, N. Y., is' one of the most elaborately finished, appropriately and comfortably furnished, and inviting resorts in which to spend a pleasant hour that we know of in the City of Churches. Its walls are adorned with many choice productions of the painter's art, of which we may mention "The Animals coming out of the Ark" and "Leander swimming across the Hellespont." Mark Hartmann is the proprietor of this elegant retreat, and over his bar are dispensed the best of liquors and the finest foreign and domestic cigars, at the most reasonable prices.

Bathing.

A very large proportion of the visitors to Coney Island find the source of their greatest pleasure in the surf-bathing. There is little to choose in the matter of location, as from one extremity of the island to the other, the beach is equally smooth and safe, and the magnificent surf of the same character. The uniform price for the use of a bathing-house and dress is 25 cents, but at a few places toward the west end, 15 or 20 cents only is charged, but 25 cents is the maximum price at the best places. At the Manhattan Beach Bathing Pavilion, Brighton Beach Bathing Pavilion, and at the Iron Pier will be found the most luxurious bathing facilities. The bathing dress should be made of a woolen fabric, as it retains the heat of the body, and therefore prevents a too rapid evaporation. Maroon and blue are the proper colors, as they resist the corrosive and bleaching effects of the salt-water. A broad-brimmed straw hat may be worn, but all cover (such as oil skin caps, so commonly worn to prevent the hair from being wet) preventing a free perspiration on the scalp, are injurious. Do not bathe just after a meal, or when over-fatigued, chilly or over-heated, or (unless with the sanction of your physician) when suffering from any acute disease, or laboring under any organic affection.

The proper time to bathe is, when in a healthful condition, when comfortably warm, two to four hours after meals, at any time between 7 a. m. and 9 p. m., from the beginning of June to the end of September. The best time is during high water. Fifteen minutes should be the average duration of a bath. One bath a day is enough for most people, although robust people may occasionally enter twice a day unharmed, and extraordinary people as often as they please. Children should never be forced to bathe. All the good effects which are expected from the bathing are nullified by the fright and nervous shock. The proper way is to get them gradually accustomed to the sea; to let them have their bathing clothes on, and play on the beach, when they will go to the edge of the water, and by-and-by find their own way in. Do not undress and dash into the water after a long walk or run, or when much heated. Do not enter the water when the stomach is entirely empty nor when you are fatigued by hard mental or physical labor. The most common cause of cramps in the legs or arms is due to ignorance of or neglect of these simple precautions. Do not go into the water sooner than two or three hours after a hearty meal, as it interferes with digestion and nullifies any good to be obtained by the exercise. For beginners especially do not stay in the water too long. Ten minutes, or at most, twenty, will be enough for one not accustomed to the water.

Coney Island Street Directory.

Boulevard (Ocean Parkway) begins at the Atlantic Ocean, and runs N. to Prospect Park, 5½ miles.

Brighton Place begins at the Creek, 200 feet W. of the Boulevard, and runs S. to the Elevated R. R.

Concourse, first avenue N. of the Ocean, runs from Hotel Brighton to P. P. & C. I. R. R. Depot.

Coney Island Road begins at Van Sicklen's Hotel, on Shell Road, and runs East to the Creek, and continues to Brooklyn. Horse cars run on this road.

Courtland Street begins at Coney Island Road, about 300 feet East of Culver's R. R. and runs South to the Sheepshead Bay Road.

Culver's Plaza, the grounds South of the P. P. & C. I. R. R. Depot.

Duck Hill, portion of Coney Island Road East of the Boulevard.

Henry Street begins at Coney Island Road opp. Brighton Chapel, and runs N. to the Creek.

Horse Car Road begins at the Concourse (Aquarium), and runs N. to the Coney Island Road. Horse Cars use this road.

New Street begins at Culver's R. R. and runs West about 500 feet, being between Coney Island Road and Sheepshead Bay road.

Ocean Avenue, first walk North of the ocean, runs from Feltman's Hotel West, about 1,000 feet.

Ocean Parkway, for location see Boulevard.

Point Road, first road S. of the Creek, runs W. from Gunther's R. R. to the point on the meadows.

Railroad Avenue begins at Coney Island Road opposite Voorhies Place, and runs S. to the Elevated R. R.

Sea Beach Walk, in front of Sea Beach Palace Hotel, runs S. from Surf Avenue to the Ocean.

Sea Breeze Avenue begins at Horse Car Road, and runs East to and along S. side of Race Track.

Shell Road runs from Creek, South to Oceanic Hotel.

Sheepshead Bay Road runs from Shell Road (Oceanic Hotel) East to East side of race track.

Surf Avenue, first road N. of the ocean, runs from P. P. & C. I. R. R. Depot West to the Point.

Surf Walk, first Walk North of the ocean, runs from Culver's Plaza to Feltman's Hotel.

Van Sicklen Place begins at the Creek, 500 feet W. of the Boulevard, and runs S. to Coney Island road.

Voorhies Place begins at the Creek, 800 feet W. of the Boulevard, and runs S. to Coney Island Road.

West Avenue, first avenue S. of the Creek, runs W. from the Boulevard, to Voorhies Place.

CONEY ISLAND.

A Classified List of Business Houses.

— • • • —

Amusements, Places of
BAUER'S W. BRIGHTON CASINO, W. Brighton
Burgarz G., Surf av., W. Brighton
COLOSSAL ELEPHANT (Joseph McCaddon, manager), Surf av., W. Brighton
Cyclorama (The), opp. Sea Beach Hotel, W. Brighton
Ceorama Camera Obscura, Culver's plaza, W. Brighton
Jenkins C. E., Ocean av.,W. Bghtn
Metropolitan Pavilion, W. 10th, W. Brighton
Observatory & Signal Co., Culver's plaza, W. Brighton
SEA BEACH PALACE EXHIBITION, W. 10th. W. Brighton
Sea Side Museum, Surf av., W. Br.
Toboggan Slide, Culver's plaza, W. Brighton
WILSON & COLMAN'S MUSEUM, Surf av. nr.W. 8th, W. Brighton

——o——

Bakers.
Baas Berend, Shell rd., W. Bright'n
POUCH ALFRED H. Van Sicklen Station
Sichling Fr., Brighton pl. nr. Boul.

——o——

Bathing Pavilions.
Bailey Daniel, W. End
DOYLE JAMES Culver's plaza W. Brighton
Hahn Chas., Ocean av.,W. Bright'n
Leopold L., nr. Old Iron Pier, W. Brighton
Lewis Warren H., W. End
Scoville J., Ocean av., W. Brighton
Stratton & Henderson, Ocean av., W. Brighton

Tilyou P. A., W. End
Van Bergen C., Ocean av.,W. Br.
VOORHIES JOHN V. Bauer's Casino, W. Brighton

——o——

Blacksmith.
O'LOAN JAMES J. 8th nr. Surf av., W. Brighton

——o——

Boarding Houses.
Corlies E. S., Boulevard c. W. av.
Delaney Mary, Brighton pl. nr. Boulevard
Moore Ann, Brighton pl., W. Br.
Sexton John A., Culver's rd.,W. Br.
Steffen Hugo, Surf av., W. Br.
VAN BERGEN SUSAN A. Surf av., W. Brighton

——o——

Boot & Shoe Maker.
Schulze P., Sea Breeze av. nr.W.3d

——o——

Boot & Shoe Dealer.
ROSENBERG LEWIS, Sea Breeze av. nr. W. 3d

——o——

Bottlers.
Buchman A. D., Surf av., W. Br.
Immerschitt H., Surf av., W. Br.
Robinson Robert, Brighton Beach
Schweickert P., Van Sicklen Sta'n
Thimig Herman, Boulevard n. Coney Island horse car rd.
VANDERVEER GEORGE, Surf av., W. Brighton

——o——

Brewers.
BUDWEISER BREWING CO. Sheepshead Bay rd., W. Br.

Brewers.

Belows Fr., Surf av., W. Brighton
Erzinger Frank, Boulevard e. Coney Island, horse car rd.
Kahn Morris, Sea Breeze av.W. 1st
Pleger H., Brighton pl. nr. Boul'd
Skinner Geo., Surf av., W. Brigh'n
Winne Th., Shell rd., W. Brighton

———0———

Carpenters & Builders

Goldstone & Brewster, Brighton pl. nr. Boulevard
Spence & Cody, W. 8th nr. Surf av. W. Brighton

———0———

Champagne.

FRASH & CO. (Champagne, &c.), at Champagne Pavilion, W. Brighton, between the Iron Piers and adjoining Paul Bauer's Hotel

———0———

Cigar Dealers.

Edler J., Iron Pier Walk, W. Br.
Hanson A. J., W. 1st nr. Boulevard
Kelly B., W. 1st nr. Sea Breeze av.

———0———

Clothing Dealer.

Gottlieb L., W. 8th nr. Surf av., W. Brighton & Sea Breeze av.

———0———

Coal & Wood.

Sanford F. S. & Co., Coney Island creek nr. Shell rd.
Ziegler & Thompson, Coney Island creek nr. Shell rd. bridge

———0———

Contractor.

Lannon M., W. 5th nr. Sea Breeze av., W. Brighton

———0———

Dentist.

Best J. H., Surf av., W. Brighton

———0———

Druggists.

Chambers A., Surf av. e. W. 8th, W. Brighton
JACKSON PHILO, Surf av., W. Brighton

Dry Goods.

Blume R., Sea Breeze av. n. Boul'd
Strauss M., Sea Breeze av. nr.W.3d

———0———

Express.

REMSEN WM. Surf av., W Brighton

———0———

Fish Dealers.

Emmens & Co., Surf av., W. Br.
Lundy Bros., Boulevard nr. Coney Island, horse car rd.

———0———

Fruit Dealers.

Brandi Bros., Iron Pier wk., W.Br.
Sessa F., Surf av., W. Brighton
Sevri Andrew, W. 5th e. Sea Breeze av., W. Brighton

———0———

Gas Companies.

Brighton Gas Light Co., W. 8th, W. Brighton
Coney Island Fuel & Gas Light Co. Brighton pl., W. Brighton

———0———

Gents Furnish'g Goods

Richter S., Sea Breeze av. nr.W. 3d

———0———

Grocers.

Baas B., Surf av. & Shell rd.,W.Br.
Clear T., Sea Breeze av. nr. W. 3d
Ditmas E. H., Brighton pl. nr.Boul
Hart & Bro., Brighton pl. nr. Boul.
JOHNSTON BROS. Brooklyn & Gravesend
Woolsey C. L., Surf av., W. Brigh'n

———0———

Hairdressers.

Burtrand Joseph,W. 5th nr. Sheepshead Bay rd., W. Brighton
Eberdardt W.V., Surf av., W. Br.
Little John, Sheepshead Bay rd.nr. W. 3d, W. Brighton
Weissenburger J., W. 1st nr. Sea Breeze av.

———0———

Hay & Straw.

Reuschenberg Richard, Coney Island, horse car rd. nr. Boulevard

Hotels.

Abbot T. C., W. 5th e. Sea Breeze av., W. Brighton
Arlington House, W. 8th W. Br.
ATLANTIC, Boulevard opp. race track
BADER C. A. Boulevard nr. Concourse
CLARENDON, (J. R. Rockfeller, prop.), W. Brighton
Cook J. A., Surf av., W. Brighton
Dixon T. I., Brighton Beach
DOYLE & STUBENBORD, Culver's plaza, W. Brighton
Fredericks Lena, Brighton pl., W. Brighton
GRAND UNION HOTEL W. 5th nr. Sea Breeze av., W. Br. the largest family hotel on the beach. Accomodation for 400. Sammells & LaBrie, props.
Hanlon T., Surf av., W. Brighton
GOOD HOME HOTEL & RESTAURANT (Aug. Samuel, prop.), Surf av. opp. Big Elephant
Hotel Boulevard, Boulevard opp. race track
HOTEL BRIGHTON, Brighton Beach
MANHATTAN BEACH, Manhattan Beach
Michel C., Sheepshead Bay rd. nr. W. 5th, W. Brighton
ORIENTAL, Manhattan Beach
Quigley J. F., Boulevard opp. the Race Track
SEA BEACH PALACE, W. Brighton
Thompson Louisa. W. 5th nr. Sea Breeze av., W. Brighton
Valentine W., Boulevard nr. Concourse
VANDERVEER WM. Surf av. W. Brighton
WEST BRIGHTON BEACH, Surf av., W. Brighton

———o———

Ice Cream.

HORTON J. M. Van Sickler Station

———o———

Laundries.

Carr Jennie, Sheepshead Bay rd. nr. W. 3d, W. Brighton
Goldsboro J., Van Sicklen station
Holmes M., W. 3d nr. S'head Bay rd.

Liquors.

Bass James, Surf av. W. Brighton
Beck C., Boulevard opp. race track
BERGER W. Boulevard opp. race track
Berkovits K., W. 5th nr. Sea Breeze av., W. Brighton
Boldt E., W. 1st nr. S'head Bay rd.
Boyd S., Sheepshead Bay rd. nr. W. 5th, W. Brighton
Briordy P., Ocean av., W. Brighton
Brooks J. S., Surf av., W. Brighton
Casey James, W. End
Cohn B., Surf av., W. Brighton
Cook A., Sea Breeze av. nr. W. 3d
Corson B. F., Boulevard nr. Coney Island, horse car rd.
Daniels J., Boulev'd opp. race track
DeNoble E. W., 3d nr. Sheepshead Bay rd.
DOYLE JOHN, W. End
Duffy P., Iron Pier walk, W. Br.
Dwyer R., Boulev'd opp. race track
Ehlers & Ballon. Ocean av., W. Br.
Eustis J. A., Sheepshead Bay rd. e. W. 3d, W. Brighton
Feltman C. W. 10th, W. Brigh'on
Fischer M., W. 5th n. Sea Breeze av. W. Brighton
FLYNN J. J. Surf av., W. Br.
FRASH & CO. Bauer's Casino, W. Brighton
Freeman A., Boulevard opp. race track
Fulton M., S'head Bay rd. e. W. 1st
COLDSMITH & PERRY, Ocean av., W. Brighton
Gorman Joseph, W. End
Groll J., Sea Breeze av. nr. W. 3d
Hart & Keys, Surf av. nr. Culver's rd., W. Brighton
Holser A., Surf av., W. Brighton
KATEN G. W. End
Klein & Seyfried. Boulevard opp. race track
KLEIST C. F. Boulevard nr. Coney Island, horse car rd.
Knight Bros., W. 8th, W. Brighton
Kuhn E. A., W. 8th, W. Brighton
Leary John, W. End
LeBlanc & Sutherland, Sea Breeze av. nr. W. 1st
Lewis J. E., Surf av., W. Brighton
Lewis W. H., Ocean av., W. Brighton
Lohman Annie, W. End.
Losee G., Ocean av., W. Brighton
Losee G. P., Boulevard opp. race track
Lyman & Vanderveer, Surf av., W. Brighton
Martin F., Sheepshead Bay rd. nr. W. Brighton
Maucher R., W. 1st nr. Boulevard
McDonald P., Sea Br'ze av. e. W. 1st
Michels J. W. 5th e. Sheepshead Bay rd., W. Brighton

Morson C., W. 5th e. Sea Breeze av.
W. Brighton
Mortimer T. A., W. End
Murray R., Surf av., W. Brighton
Myers J. C., Surf av., W. Brighton
Nana Frederick, W. End
Nebendahl C.,W.3d nr. Sheepshead
Bay rd., W. Brighton
Olney T. P., Surf av.,W. Brighton
PALMETTO (THE), Wine &
Lunch Room under Paul Bauer's,
W. Brighton (Edward Heidman,
prop.)
Perry S., W. 1st nr. Sea Breeze av.
Pettigrove J., W. 10th,W. Brighton
Popper H., Sea Breeze av. e. W. 1st
Rauscher Martin, W. End
Ravenhall Richard, W. End
Reeber F., W. 10th, W. Brighton
Rogers L., Culver's rd.W. Brighton
Ryan T., Surf av., W. Brighton
Samuel A., Surf av., W. Brighton
Schaefer L. W.,5th nr. Sea Breeze
av., W. Brighton
Schweickert P., Iron Pier Walk, W.
Brighton
Skinner G., Surf av., W. Brighton
Stillwell J. H., Van Sicklen Station
Stratton & Henderson, Ocean av.,
W. Brighton
STRUBE H. Surf av.,W. Brigh'n
Stubenbord J. G., W. End
Van Strydonck J. B., Surf av., W.
Brighton
Wagner E., W. 10th, W. Brighton
Welch D., W. Brighton
**WENDLKEN & NISTER-
MANN,** Surf av. e. W. 8th, W.
Brighton
Williams G. H., W. 5th e. Sheeps-
head Bay rd., W. Brighton
Williams J., Surf av., W. Brighton

———o———

Milk, Butter, Etc.

Overton C. C., Brighton pl., W. Br.
Rehazeek F., Bauer's Casino,W.Br.

———o———

Notaries Public.

Morris C. E., W. 8th nr. Surf av.
Overton C. C., Brighton pl.
VOORHIES S. I. W. 8th nr.
Surf av., W. Brighton

— o —

Photographers.

Abraham, Bauer's Casino, W. Br.
Abraharns D., Brighton Beach
COLE C. Culver's plaza, W. Br.
Gallagher, Iron Pier Walk, W. Br.
Williams J. M., Iron Pier Walk, W.
Brighton

Plumbers.

Gallagher F. P., Surf av.,W. Brigh'n
Galvin J. W., 8th nr. Surf av., W.
Brighton
McEntire M. F., Sheepshead Bay
rd. nr. W. 6th, W. Brighton

———o———

Real Estate Agents.

ABBOTT THOMAS C. W.
5th e. Sea Breeze av., W. Brighton
CONWAY JAMES J.
Brighton pl. n. Van Sicklen Sta'n
Waring & Bader, Surf av., W. Br.

———o———

Restaurants.

Behr J., W. Brighton
BRAXTON E. W. 3d nr. Sheeps-
head Bay rd.
Brody & Osterberg, Ocean av., W.
Brighton
Davenport G. R., Ocean av. W. Br.
FISHER L. G. Surf av. e. W. 8th
W. Brighton
Gerhardt L., Ocean av., W. Brigh'n
Lampe E., Surf av., W. Brighton
McCANN P. H. Surf av.,W. Br.
Milli P., Surf av., W. Brighton
Mott L., Sea Beach Walk, W. Br.
MULLER W. Culver's plaza, W.
Brighton
Redmond, Surf av., W. Brighton
Schiffman C., W. 10th, W. Brighton
Smith W. L., N. 10th,W. Brighton
Valentine Bros., Ocean av., W. Br.

———o———

Shooting Galleries.

Boolzen C., Iron Pier Walk, W. Br.
HOULAHAN J. Culver's plaza,
W. Brighton
Jansen W., Surf av., W. Brighton
Langcake J., Brighton Beach
Moe A., Surf av.,W. Brighton

———o———

Soda & Mineral Waters.

Goldberger, Surf av., W. Brighton
Rich J. E., Sea Beach Walk, W. Br.
SCHULTZ C. H. W. 1st nr.
Boulevard

———o———

Wine Domestic.

FRASH & CO. Champagne
Etc. Champagne Pavilion, W. Br.
Beach between the Irons Piers,
& adjoinging Paul Bauer's Hotel

BATH BEACH.

A Classified List of Business Houses.

——·•·——

Agent, News.
Emrich J., Bath av. e. Gunther's rd.

——o——

Agents, Insurance.
Young & Fergueson, Bath av. e. Plank rd.

——o——

Agents, Real Estate.
MORRISEY W. G. & CO.
Cropsey av. e. Old Plank rd.
Young & Furgneson. Bath av. e. Plank road

——o——

Baker.
Koster J., 18th nr. Benson av.

——o——

Boarding Houses.
Avoca Villa, Mrs. Rosenberg.
BATH BEACH HOUSE,
(T. Lewers), Cropsey av.
Cozine M. A., Benson av. e. 18th av.
Cromwell W. H., DeBruyn's la. e. R. R.
Davis B. A., 19th av. e. Bath av.
Finn J., Bath av. & 13th av.
Fisher's Cottage, Benson av. nr. DeBruyn's la.
FLORENCE HOUSE,
(P. J. Flannagan), Cropsey av. e. Bay 17th av.
Franklin House, Crosby av. e. Bay 13th
Franklin Mrs., 22nd av. nr. R. R.
Gross J., Bay 13th nr. Bath av.
Hageman T. M., Benson av. nr. Bay 19th
Hougenot Cottage, K. Cheeseboro, Bay 17th nr. Cropsey av.
Holmes H. M., Bath av.

Lexington House, Stephen O'Brien, 18th av. nr. Bath av.
LOWRY HOUSE, (J. L. Lowry), 17th av.
May Villa, E. J., Byerly, Cropsey e. 17th av.
ORR Mrs, Bath av. e. Bay 17th
Park Cottage, J. T., Hayes, Cropsey av. e. 18th av.
Sadler H. M., Cropsey av.
San-Soucí Villa, Mrs. Humphrey, Cropsey nr. Plank rd.
Stubbs Mrs. Cropsey av. & Bay 17th
Teed A. M., Bay 16th
Tubner J., DeBruyn's la.
Zeyner Villa, A. E., Thomas Bay 13th e. Cropsey av.

——o— —

Boots and Shoes.
Brady M., Benson av.
Gilbert T., Benson av. nr. Bay 17th
Rambaud E., Plank rd. nr. Bath av

——o——

Butchers.
Basiley P. D., Benson av. Plank rd.
Stern M., Plank rd. nr. Bath av.

——o——

Carpenters & Builders.
Ball J., Bath av. nr. Cropsey av.
Way & Aumack, DeBruyn's la.

——o——

Dressmakers.
Brady Miss, Bennet's la. nr. Cropsey
Holmes H. M., Bath av.

——o——

Drugs.
Bruner O. R., Old Plank rd. nr. Bath av.
Morrisey J. F., Cropsey av. e. Old Plank rd.

Dry and Fancy Goods.

BATH BEACH BAZAAR,
adjoining Postoffice

——o——

Expresses.

Guthiel F., Postoffice
Remsen W., Postoffice
Tiedge F., Postoffice

——o——

Fancy Goods·

Ball E., 18th av. nr. Benson av.
FETTRETCH K. J. 18th av.
e. Benson av.

——o——

Florists.

Quigley J., 17th av. nr. Benson av.
Schntze H., nr. Atlantic Garden

——o——

Fruit

Meyey W., 18th av. nr. Benson av.
Roth M., 18th av. nr. Benson av.

——o——

Grocers.

Gerekin J. C., Bath av. e. DeBruyn's la.
Wolff & Moore, 18th av. e. Benson av.
Wright W. H., & Co. Benson av. nr. 18th av.

——o——

Hairdresser.

Brunner J., Plank rd. nr. Bath av.

——o——

Hardware.

Ball E., 18th av. nr. Bath av.

——o——

Hotels.

Arens H., Plank rd. e. Cropsey av.
Atlantic, F. B., Furnell, Bath av. nr. 19th av.
AVON BEACH (Geo. Shields), Cropsey av. nr. Bay 19th
Idle Rest, Frederick Semken, ft. Plank rd
Keystone House, Herman Kirstein, Cropsey av. e. 20th av.
Willomere Place, Cropsey nr. Bay 17th

Ice Cream.

Bosch Teressa, Bath av. nr. R. R. Depot

——o——

Lawyer.

Cropsey A. G., Main e. Bay 16th, P. O. Box 13

——o——

Liquors.

Hornet John J., Cropsey av. e. 19th av.
Sanders R. W., Plank rd. e. Benson av.
Stehlin Joseph, Bath av.

——o——

Livery Stable.

Shields G., 19th av. nr. Cropsey av.

——o——

Milkmen.

Hogan M., Bennet's la. nr. Bath av.
Lundy J. E., Cropsey av. & Plank rd

——o——

Painter.

Ashton J. M., Benson av.

——o——

Physician.

Ward J., Bay 16th nr. Benson av.

——o——

Plumber.

Clinch J., Bay 13th e. Bath av.

——o——

Schools.

Curley E., 17th av.
VILLA DE SALES ACAD. (Female), New Utrecht la.

——o——

Telegraph Companies.

Baltimore & Ohio, Railroad Depot
Western Union, Avon Beach Hotel

——o——

Telephone Companies.

N. Y. & New Jersey, Cropsey av. e. Old Plank rd. Call 800 A.

FORT HAMILTON.

A Classified List of Business Houses.

◆◆

Boarding Houses.
NORTON C. E. Stewart av.

———o———

Boats to Let.
GATES P. & M. Shore rd. nr. Stewart av.
Hegeman R. H., ft. Stewart av.
Stillwell Adrian, shore rd. nr. Fort Hamilton av.

———o———

Blacksmiths.
Lake J., Jonh nr. Stewart av.

———o———

Boots & Shoes.
Kluge H., 5th av. nr. 86th
Rupprecht P., Stewart av. nr. Clark

———o———

Butcher.
Costello P., Stewart av. c. Wasn'n av.
Mittnight F., 91st nr. 4th av.

———o———

Carpenters.
Doyle M., 91st & 4th av.
Emmons R., Denyse nr. Stewart av.
Hastings & Albers, Fort Hamilton av. nr. 92nd
Jones J. R., 89th nr. 5th av.
Tierny W. J., 91st nr. 3d av.

———o———

Carriage Makers.
Penger W. E., 86th nr. Fort Hamilton av.
Stadler Joseph, Forest pl nr. 4th av.

Cigar Dealers.
Mehl C., 5th av. c. 91st
Meyer F., Fort Hamilton av. c. Laf.

———o———

Confectioners.
Finley M., Fort Hamilton av. nr. Shore rd.
FLYNN A. 5th av. nr. 91st

———o———

Contractor.
McGlyn J., Church nr. Stewart av.
Mitchell W., Stewart av. nr. 4th av.

———o———

Country Stores.
Berry A., Stewart av. c. Clarke.
BURTON T. Forest pl. nr. 4th av.
EMMONS R. Denyse nr. Stewart av.
Slater R., Stewart av. nr. Gates.
Tasso M., 92nd nr. 3d av.

———o———

Dressmakers.
Meyer J., Fort Hamilton av. c. Laf.
Rice B., 92nd nr. Concord

———o———

Druggists.
BLANKLEY W. H. Stewart. av. c. Clarke

———o———

Expresses.
McKnight Michael, Stewart av. c. Laf
WESTAWAY WILLIAM A. Clarke nr. Stewart av.

Fish.

Richman A. G., Warren c. Laf.
Smith W. J., Stewast av. nr. Church

---0---

Fancy Goods.

McCLYN M. A. Stewart av. c.
Church
Molloy M., 4th av. c. 88th

---0---

Fruits.

Monahan J., Warren nr. 92nd

---0---

Furnished Rooms.

CLAPP MRS. H. H. c. Shore
Road & 3d av.

---0---

Grocers.

Bock Elizabeth, 91st nr. 3d av.
Clarke W., 5th av. c. Prospect pl.
FARRELL M. 3d av. nr. 91st
Folsom M. A., Gibson av. nr. 92nd
KELLY J. Fort Hamilton av. c.
Church
Lake A. A., Stewart av. c. John
MULLER W. 5th av. c. 89th
Otten A., 5th av. nr. 91st
Parker M., Fort Hamilton av. nr.
Clarke

---0---

Hairdressers.

Folsom S. M., Clarke nr. Stewart av.

---0---

Hotels.

Bay View House, James Keegan,
Shore rd.
Brooklyn House, John J., Walsh,
Stewart av. nr. Denyse
DYKER HOUSE, G., Duryea.
NEW DYKER, G., Bierlein,
Shore rd.
Grand View
Haas O., 86th nr. Town Hall
Live Oak, 92nd c. Concord
Newnrn House, J., Hunt, Stewart
av. c. Denyse
Ocean Hotel, H. B., Johnson, Fort
Hamilton av. c. Shore rd.
UNITED STATES, Michael
Gates, Shore rd. nr. Stewart av.
SEA VIEW, John Nappier,
Shore rd. nr. Fort Hamilton

Ice Dealers.

Brady P., 90th nr. 4th av.
Clark T. J., 5th av. nr. 83th
McNally Bros. Clarke nr. Stewart
av.

---0---

Liquors.

Burke Patrick, 92d nr. Concord
Drury J., Denyse nr. Stewart av.
DUFFY F. 92nd nr. Concord
Kirk J. W., Fort Hamilton av. nr.
Gates
Leydet J., Fort Hamiltyn av. c.
Church
Mang F., 92nd nr. 4th av.
Martin H., Denyse nr. Stewars av.
Monaghan M., Warren nr. Laf.
Jemsen M., 5th av. c. Forest pl.
SMITH J. F. 86th nr. Fort Ham-
ilton av.
Taylor J. P., 4th av. c. Lex. av.
White E., Lex. av. nr. 3d av.
Willis J. H., Fort Hamilton av. nr.
Clarke
WYNNE J. B. 3d av. nr. 91st

---0---

Mason.

McGlynn J., Stewart ax. c. Church

---0---

Milk.

Coyle P., Warren nr. 92nd
Hickman T., 91st nr. 4th av.

---0---

Nurse.

McBride M., 3d av. nr. Lex. av.

---0---

Oils.

Carroll L., Warren nr. Lex. av.

---0---

Photographers.

COLE C. R. opp. United States
Hotel

---0---

Tailors.

GOODWIN J. 92nd nr. Warren
Katzenberger J., Concord na. 92nd
Ott W., Forest pl. nr. 4th av.

---0---

Telegraph Cos.

Western Union, Stewart av. n. John

SHEEPSHEAD BAY.

A Classified List of Business Houses.

Amusement Places of.

Coney Island Jockey Club, Sheepshead Bay Race Course, Ocean av.

———o———

Boarding Houses.

Allen Mrs., Voorheis nr. Ocean av.
Costigan Mrs., Anthony nr. Voorheis av.
EATON VILLA, Mrs. E. Burns, props. Voorheis av. House & Cuisine strictly first class.
Fitzpatrick Mrs., Anthony nr. Voorheis av.
Gordon Villa, Mrs. Gordon, Ocean av. nr. Shore rd.
Hallenbeck Mrs., Anthony nr. Voorheis av.
Head Mrs., Voorheis nr. Bay rd.
Ivy Villa, Jacob Sauer, Ocean av. nr. Shore rd.
Lothrop A., Bay rd. Voorheis av.
MACKS VILLA, Private Boarding House, Ocean av. Second House e. Voorheis la. Letter Box 76
MANHATTAN VILLA, J. L. Hawley, Bay rd.
Ocean Villa, Mrs. Caroline McDivet Ocean av. nr. Voorheis
Oriental House, Stephen Teets, Bay rd.
Renwick House & Cottage, D., Teets Bay rd. nr. Voorheis av.
Rose Cottege, T., McKeon, Neck rd. nr. Manhattan R. R.
Seaside Villa, Job Young, Ocean av. nr. Shore rd.
ST. ELMO VILLA, E. A. Mason Bay rd.
Sullivan Mrs., Ocean nr. Voorheis av.
The Brunswick, Mrs. G. Worden, Bay rd.
White D. (Huisman's Hotel), Bay rd.

Boat Builders.

Esmark W., Shore rd.
PACE JOSEPH A. Shore rd. nr. Anthony

———o———

Boats to Let.

Colwell J., Shore rd.
DICK J. C. Shore rd.
Tappan G. C., Shore rd. nr. Anthony

———o———

Boots & Shoes.

Sumner C. T., Bay rd. nr. Manhattan R. R. Station

———o———

Von Fricken Fritz, Anthony & Dunooley la.

———o———

Butchers.

Huisman R., Shore rd.
Kahn C., Anthony nr. Shore rd.

———o———

Carpenters.

Anmack O. S., Anthony
McKane J. Y., Voorheis av. e. E. 22nd

———o———

Cigar Dealers.

Healy M., E. 13th
Schuessler C., Bay rd. nr. Brighton R. R. Station

———o———

Confectionery.

Havemeyer H. E., 13th nr. X av.
Healy M., E. 13th
Loesins Leo. Bay rd.
SCHUESSLER C. Bay rd.

Druggists.

Burrows A., Teet's row
KITCHEN'S PHARMACY,
Shore rd. nr. Voorheis av.

---o---

Dry Goods.

BARRETT ELLEN E. Bay rd.
e. Manhattan R. R. Station
SHALMOVITZ D. Shore rd. e.
Ocean av.
Vander N. E., Manhattan R. R.
Station

---o---

Express.

Long Island, Manhattan R. R. St.

---o---

Fish.

Lundy Brothers, Shore rd. opp.
Dooley la.

---o---

Grocers.

Huisman A., Anthony ar. Shore rd.
McKANE R. Anthony nr. Shore
rd.
McKeon B. & Son, Bay rd.
ULMAN A. Anthony nr. Shore
rd.

---o---

Hairdressers.

Nissen C. M., Island view Hotel.
White J. M., Anthony nr. Shore rd.

---o---

Hardware.

McKANE G. D. Dooleys la.

---o---

Horseshoer.

Barrett W., Bay rd.

---o---

Hotels.

Adelphi, W., Schuessler, Brighton
R. R. Station
ATLANTIC, Ellen McMachon,
Shore rd. nr. Ocean av.
Cordes Jacob, Cordes Hotel, Shore
rd. e. Anthony
Huismans A., Huismans, Shore rd.
HOTEL JEROME, Mrs. J. C.,
Gilbert, Shore rd.

Island View, Henry Grauel, Man-
hattan R. R. Station
Manhattan Cottage, M. Purcell,
Shore rd.
Ocean Villa, M. J. Mead, Bay rd.
OSBORN'S H., Osborn, Shore
rd. nr. Ocean av.
Schroder & Kronika, Anthony nr.
Shore rd.
Sheepsh'd Bay Hotel, J. A. Balmer,
Ocean av. e. Shore av.
TAPPEN'S, G. C. Tappan, Shore
nr. Anthony
United States, P. J., Murtagh, Bay
rd.
Washington Hotel, W. H. Harland
Bay rd.

---o---

Ice Cream.

LOESING LEO, Bay rd.

---o---

Liquors.

Alter H., Shore rd. e. Ocean av.
Boyle A. Bay rd. nr. Brighton Beach
R. R.
COSGROVE T. nr. Manhattan
R. R.
Gorman J. E. 13th e. Snipe
Guinan M., E. 14th e. X av.
McMahon J., E. 15th nr. Emma la.
McMAHON THOMAS, Man-
hattan R. R. Station

---o---

Laundries.

McKinley Mary E., 16th nr. Bay
Newport J., Vander Noot, Manhattan R. R. Station

---o---

Painters.

ANDREWS W. Anthony nr.
Shore rd.
FLINN A. T. House Painters &
Interior Decorator, P. O. Box 49
Seyers A., Anthony nr. Shore rd.

---o---

Plumbers.

Clarke R., Bay rd.
Hallstead J., Dooley

---o---

Real Estate Agents.

Burtis J., Ocean av. nr. Shore rd.
Summer C. T., Bay rd. Teet's row
Vander N. J., Manhattan R. R.

ROCKAWAY BEACH.

A Classified List of Business Houses.

— • • —

Amusements Places of.
Allens Museum, Allen & Co., Sea
Side Station
Kingsland Casino, M. Kingsland,
Sea Side Station

—o—

Barbers.
Jackson A., Hammel Station
Kummer E., Grove av.

—o—

Bathing Pavilions.
Dun K. S., Sea side station
Wainright & Smith Sea Side Station

—o—

Boarding Houses.
CLOSS Mrs P. Bet. Beach av.
& Holland
FAILING H. on the Ocean opp.
Neptune R. R. Station

—o—

Boats to Let.
Carle J., Hammel Station

—o—

Bottlers.
Bennett G., Hammel Station

—o—

Butchers.
Murray Bros., Hammel Station

—o—

Cottages.
Jefferson Cottage, Hammel Station
KINGS COTTAGE, Hammel
Station

Druggists.
Link C. H., Hammel Station

—o—

Dry Goods.
Kohn J., Hammel Station

—o—

Grocers.
Jennings W., Hammel Station
Pearsall & Fisher, Hammel Station
Sprague Bros., Sea Side Station

—o—

Hotels.
Arlington House, Mrs. E. Claus, Sea
Side Station
Atlantic House, J. Bowe, Sea Side
Station
ATLAS HOTEL, J. J. Curley,
Sea Side Station
BALDWINS, F. Baldwins,
Hammel Station
Belvedere, A. Meesel, Hammel
Station
Bessler F., Atlantic Park
Boulevard, H. Sturm, Hammel
Station
Columbia Grove House, A. Smith,
Sea Side R. R. av. & Eldert Grove
Columbia House, H. Kruse, Sea Side
Station
Cosmopolitan, J. Merkle
Cottage Home, J. Whyte, Hammel
Station
East End Pavilion, E. Rambo, Ham-
mel Station
ELDERTS, L. ELDERT,
Hammel Station
Fishermans Inn, G. Fuchs, Ham-
mel Station
GRAND REPUBLIC, Weis-
koff & Levy, Sea Side Station
Grand Union, E. L. Morrison, Sea
Side Station

GROBES PAVILION,
Holland Station
Grotz's, W. Grotz, Hammel Station

HAMMEL'S, W. Wenkhoff,
Hammel Station

HANOVER HOUSE, L. A..
Woolenwebers, bet. Sea Side &
Neptune Station
Highland House, G. A. Sherman,
Hammel Station
Hoffman House, J. Hoffman, Sea
Side Station
Hotel Stuttgart, H. Hillmeyer, Sea
Side Station
Hunters Home, J. Kreuscher,
Hammel Station

**MADIGANS N. Y. PAVIL-
ION,** Neptune Station
Martin House, R. T. Martin, Ham-
mel Station

METROPOLITAN HOUSE,
J. Bretz's, Hammel Station

MEYER'S PAVILION, S.
Meyer, Hammel Station

NEPTUNE HOUSE, J. H.
Fisher, Neptune Station
Ocean House, L. Lang, Ocean av.
Ocean House, P. Magerus, Ham-
mel Station
Ocean Pavilion, F. Welch, Ocean
av.
Ocean & Bay View House, M. Geary
Rockaway Pier House, F. Page, Sea
Side Station

**RULANDS SEA SIDE PAV-
ILION** A. Ruland, Hammel
Station

SEA BEACH PAVILION, C.
B. Skinner, Sea Side av. Sea Side
Station
Schuster W., Sea Side Station
Seamans, R. Seamans, Sea Side
Station
Sea Side House, G. S. Barkentin
Sea Side Station
Summit House, J. W. Rosebrook
Hammel Station
The Capitol, Foley & Co., Sea Side
Station

Williamsburgh Hotel, W. Collins,
Sea Side Station

ROCKAWAY, S. Meyers & T.
Pape Supts, Sea Side Station

———o———

Liquors.

Bay Shore House, G. H. Appleby,
Hammel Station
Harrison S. G., Hammel Station
Henne W., Sea Side Station
Magerus M., Hammel Station
Rau G., Hammel Station
Remsen J. H., Sea Side Station
Smith G. W., Sea Side Station

———o———

Livery Stables.

Skinner H. W., Henry St. & L. I.
R. R.
Tenau R., Sea Side Station

———o———

Pavilion.

MAMOTH, Murray & Valentine
Sea Side Station

———o———

Plumbers.

ENSCOE J. & BRO. Neptune
Station
Hough & Kupper, Hammel Station

———o———

Restaurants.

Gravelins H. C., Hammel Station
New England Kitchen, Sea Side
Station

———o———

Sanitarium.

SEA SIDE SANITARIUM,
Hammel Station

A Classified List of Business Houses.

Agents (Patent.)
SERRELL LEMUEL W. 140
Nassau

—o—

Air Compressors.
INGERSOLL ROCK DRILL CO. 10 Park pl.
RAND DRILL CO. 23 Park pl.

—o—

Ale Importers.
LOCKWOOD & GEERY
Bass' Ale, London Porter & Guinness' Stout), 165 Front

—o—

Annuciators.
ZIMARDS C. E. & CO. 237
Mercer

—o—

Architects.
AM. INSTITUTE OF ARCHITECTS, 18 Broadway

—o—

Architects' & Engineer's Drawing Materials.
BRANDIS FREDERICK E. 55 Fulton
SOLTMANN E. G. (Blue process paper for sale, and large tracing copied by the Blue process. Samples of Drawing paper mailed on application), 119 Fulton

—o—

Architectural Iron Works.
CHENEY & HEWLETT, 201 Broadway

Arms & Ammunition.
HAKSLEY & GRAHAM, 17-19 Maiden la.
HODGKINS W. C. 300 B'way
WINCHESTER REPEATING ARMS CO. 312 B'way

—o—

Artist's Materials.
DEVOE F. W. & CO. 105 Fulton
KEUFFEL & ESSER, 127 Fulton and 42 Ann
KNOEFLER M. & CO. 170 Fifth av.

—o—

Awning Stripes & Materials.
BOYLE JOHN, 203 Fulton
BRINCKERHOFF, TURNER & CO. 109 Duane
MARTIN THOMAS, 316 Canal

—o—

Awning, Tent & Flag Mfrs.
SHERMAN WM. P. & CO. (also tents and canopies to let). 946 Broadway
SKELTON F. 1325 Broadway

—o—

Baby Carriage Mfrs.
YOUNG JAMES K. & CO. Manufacturers also of Rocking & Spring Horses, Velocipedes, and Patent American Trotter. 814 to 818 E. 5th

Bankers.

GRECORY, BALLOU & CO. 1 New

INTERNATIONAL BANKING CO. 160 Fulton

KELLY EUGENE & CO. 45 Exchange

LANHAM, ALEXANDER & CO. 16 Wall

LAZARD FRERES, 46 Exchange pl.

SELIGMAN J. & W. & CO. Mills bldg.

WHITE LOOMIS L. & CO. 40 Wall

———o———

Bar Fixtures.

IBA CARPER, 8 Stanton (rear)

———o———

Billiard Goods.

HARVEY WM. & CO. 392 Broadway
SHARLOW JOSEPH, 116 Fulton
TOTAN & SCHMIDT (Balls, Cues, &c.), 89 Fulton

———o———

Bitters.

ANGOSTURA BITTERS (J. W. Wuppermann, agt.), 51 B'way

———o———

Boiler Cleaners (MECHANICAL).

HOTCHKISS J. F. 93 John

———o———

Bottle Caps.

LEHMAIER, SCHWARTZ & CO. 33 to 37 Bleecker

WITTEMANN BROS. 192 Fulton

o

Bottled Beer.

BEATTY ROBERT, 11 Beach
REDLING & NEUBAUER, 523 Broadway

Brass Bedsteads.

GOULD ROBERT S. (Successor to Krickl, Gould & Co.), 432 Broadway
MESSEREAU W. T. & CO. 321 Broadway

———o———

Brewers.

ALBANY BREWING CO. 365 to 369 West
CLAUSEN H. & SON BREWING CO. 309 E. 47th
FITZGERALD BROS. 439 Washington

———o———

Bronze Powder.

AMERICAN BRONZE POWDER MFG. CO. 6 Murray
FUCHS & LANG, 29 Warren
GERSTENDORFER BROS. 17 Barclay

———o———

Brush Mfrs. & Dealers.

DEVOE F. W. & CO. 103 Fulton

———o———

Calcium Lights.

NEW YORK CALCIUM LIGHT CO. 410 Bleecker
UNEXCELLED FIRE WORKS CO. (THE), 7 to 11 Park pl.

———o———

Carriage & Coach BUILDERS.

BREWSTER J. B. & CO.

of 25th street. (Established 1838. Incorporated 1877. Sole Mfrs. of the Brewster Wagon, which command a higher price than any other make, owing to its superior qualities and finish, besides the use of vertical steel plates in axle beds & patent cross springs), Factory, 141 to 153 E. 25th; Warerooms, 5th av. c. 42d

Cigar Flavors.

CHASKEL JAMES & CO.
93 John

FRIES ALEX. & BRO. 92
Reade

——o——

Confectioners.

Manufacturers & Wholesale.

HUMBERT C. 9 Wooster

MAZZETTI LOUIS F. 873
6th av.

ROUSREAU C. 1021 6th av.

——o——

Cracker Bakers.

BRINCKERHOFF & CO.
92 to 96 Elizabeth

——o——

Demijohns.

CIANEY J. R. 43 Murray

——o——

Dumb Waiters.

MURTAUGH'S (Established
1855). **GENUINE DUMB
WAITERS,** Manufactured only
at 145-147 E. 42d, New York. Also
Hand Hoisting in all its branches.
Carriage & Safety Invalid Eleva-
tors a specialty. Repairing and
Altering on the shortest notice.'
JAS. MURTAUGH.

——o——

Elastic Stockings &
BANDAGES.

MILHAU'S J, SON (to order
at one days' notice ; the only way
to secure fresh new goods & perfect fit), 183 Broadway

——o——

Electric Gas Lighting
APPARATUS.

BOGART ABRAHAM L.
(patentee & mfr. of **ELECTRIC
GAS LIGHTING BURNERS**
for single hand or multiple gas
lighting. **HOTEL ANNUNCIA-
TORS, BURGLAR ALARMS**
& every other electric appliance
known), 22 Union sq.

Elevators.

BLASI JOHN N. 54 W.
Broadway

**MORSE, WILLIAMS &
CO.** 108 Liberty

OTIS BROS. & CO. 35 to 37
Park row & 2 to 8 Beekman

WHITTIER MACHINE CO.
91 Liberty

——o——

Engravers.
Bank-Note.

**AMERICAN BANK
NOTE CO.** (execute every
description of Bank-Note & Se-
curities, Railway Tickets, Type
& Lithographic Work), 78 to 86
Trinity pl.

**BALDWIN & GLEASON
CO.** 61 Broadway
Continental Bank Note Co., 80
Trinity pl.

**FRANKLIN BANK-NOTE
CO.** (Engravers & Printers of
Bank Notes, Bonds, Certificates
& Securities of all kinds. Rail-
way Tickets of all descriptions).
142 Broadway

——o——

Expresses.
European.

**AMERICAN, FOREIGN &
EUROPEAN EXPRESS
CO.** (Fast Freight Line, Davies
Turner & Co.), 34 Broadway

**BALDWIN'S AMERICAN,
EUROPEAN & HAVANA
EXPRESS,** 53 Broadway

CONTANSEAU L. & CO.
(Rapid Foreign Express), 128
Broadway

**DAVIES EUROPEAN EX-
PRESS** (Fast Freight Line), 34
Broadway

**HENSEL, BRUCKMANN
& LORBACHER** (**PARCEL
AGENCY OF THE IM-
PERIAL GERMAN MAIL**), 25
William

——o——

Feed Water Heater.

**BERRYMAN PATENT
FEED WATER HEATER
& PURIFIER** (B. F. Kelly,
agt.), 91 Liberty

Filters.
BOOMER & BOSCHERT PRESS CO. 219 Fulton

----o----

Fire-Proof Building
MATERIALS.
ASBESTOS PACKING CO. (THE), 33 John

----o----

Folding Beds.
$15. KING'S FOLDING Beds, 116 W. 35th Street. $1000 buys no better bed. Guaranteed twenty years

----o----

Fountains, Vases &
STATUARY.
MOTT J. L. IRON WORKS (THE), 88-90 Beekman & 147 W. 35th & 3d av. c. 133d

----o----

Frame Mfrs.
BECKER BROS. (Mfrs. of Gilt & Bronze Pictures Mouldings of every color & description for decorative purposes & the hanging of pictures, looking glass & picture frames; also dealers in Looking Glass Plates; old frames regilt equal to new), 330 W. 36th
BEERS BROS. 814 Broadway

----o----

French Fruit Glaces.
BERNARD LEO. & CO. 228 Pearl
HUMBERT C. 9 Wooster

----o----

Fruit (Foreign &
DOMESTIC).
ROSENSTEIN BROS. (Importers of foreign fruit seeds & produce, Holland herring, Norwegian stock-fish & Cod-liver oil, etc. Sole agents of Emil Roullit's celebrated French Sardine, with & without Patent Key opener. Packers of Victor Renci Domestic Sardines, Royal Brand Mustard & Spiced Sardines & Lobsters), 317-319 Greenwich

Furniture Movers.
METROPOLITAN VAN CO. (The largest "Van" Co. in the United States. Vans to all points by Road, Rail or Water). 202 to 208 & 193 Mercer

----o----

Gas Stoves.
BOGART ABRAHAM L. 22 Union sq., 4th av. side

----o----

Ginger Ale.
(IMPORTED)
N. Y. BOTTLING CO. 162 S. 5th av.
ROSS HENRY H. 32 Broadway

----o----

Glass Signs & Letters.
ASBURY GLASS SIGN CO. 41 Day
DENZI I. F. & CO. 24 Dey
HERRLEIN & CO. 122 Liberty
RODIER & FITZGERALD 302 Pearl
STIETZ OTTO, N. Y. GLASS LETTER CO. (Sole Mfrs. Patented Glass Letters & Numbers), Broome c. Bowery (See advt. top of page)

----o----

Gold Paint.
GERSTENDORFER BROS. 17 Barclay

Mrs. E. M. Van Brunt,

Dress Reform

Rooms,

No. 39 East 19th Street,

Bet. Broadway and Fourth Avenue.

———➤ ✦ ≺ ✦———

Hygienic & Artistic Clothing

FOR WOMEN AND CHILDREN.

THE UNITED STATES.

MICHAEL YATES, Proprietor.

FORT HAMILTON,

Near the Brooklyn Railroad Depot.

Commands a fine view of the Narrows and the upper and lower bays.

Special facilities for boating and fishing.

PHOTOGRAPHER.

CHARLES P. COLE,

FORT HAMILTON and CONEY ISLAND.

Any one desiring a good picture should not fail to visit one of Mr. Cole's Studios — of which he has six — two at Fort Hamilton and four at Coney Island.

ARTISTS' MATERIALS,

J. MARSCHING & CO.,

27 PARK PLACE, NEW YORK.

Importers and Dealers in Supplies for all Kinds of Art Work.

SEND FOR NEW ILLUSTRATED CATALOGUE.

ROBERT C. PURCELL,

DEALER IN

Suits, Cloaks, Dry & Fancy Goods

944 THIRD AVENUE,

Between 56th and 57th Streets, **NEW YORK.**